"Burning body fat is a key to obtaining optimal health and fitness. Dr. Lopez explains how to do it in a simple and effective way."

Dr. Philip Maffetone, author, researcher, and Founder of MAF BioNutritionals.

"Finally a simple explanation on how stress can be affecting our weight loss efforts."

Doug Kaufmann, syndicated TV host "Your Health Matters"

"An easy to comprehend book that helps people understand how stress and hormones are involved with weight loss and health."

Dr. William G. Timmins, Founder & Director, BioHealth Diagnostics

"Dr. Lopez teaches the true importance of both aerobic and anaerobic training."

Doug Atkinson, Athletic Trainer, Dallas Mavericks and Chicago Bulls

To Burn or Not to Burn, Fat is the Question!

By Dr. Len Lopez

The information and advice contained in this book are based upon the author's personal and professional experiences and are not intended to replace proper medical advice. Before beginning any health program, you should consult with your health care provider. The author is not responsible for any adverse effects resulting from the use of any principles discussed in this book.

Illustrator: Pete Grubb
Graphic Designer: Gary Bruce
Printer: Bookmasters, Inc.
Distribution: Bookmasters, Inc.

ISBN 0-9710797-0-6

Printed in the United States of America

Book Masters, Inc.
P.O. Box 388
Ashland, OH 44805
800-247-6553
order@bookmasters.com

www.DrLenLopez.com

TABLE OF CONTENTS

Introduction

If you are one of the millions of people who constantly struggle with your weight and are always on some type of diet or exercise program to help fight the battle of the bulge, this book will be very helpful to you.

Many people spend half their life dieting yet they still can't lose any weight. Some wonder why they spend so much time exercising with little or no results to show. Others claim they do a good job of dieting and exercising, but are still unable to reach their desired weight loss goals. With so much dieting and exercise we should be seeing more positive results. Unfortunately, here in America, problems with weight gain and obesity are a growing concern and never ending problem for many.

Most people think diet and exercise are all that's involved when it comes to losing weight and keeping it off. There are many people who diet properly and routinely exercise, but are still not seeing the results they want when they look in the mirror. Keep in mind that if you are dieting properly and routinely exercise, but still not losing weight or shaping up, then diet and exercise may not be the only pieces of this puzzle. Stress could be a factor!

Stress may be part of the problem that's holding back your results. Is there heavy stress in your life? Do you always feel fatigued and run down? Are you constantly on the go? Do you suffer from headaches, indigestion, bloating, constipation, allergies, PMS, menopause, arthritis, diabetes and low blood sugar? Do you get enough sleep each night? If you're answering yes to this short list of questions there is a good chance that stress is overwhelming your body and triggering hormonal responses that are working against you in your weight loss efforts, not to mention the possibility that your diet and exercise programs may be triggering the wrong hormonal responses. You could be activating all the triggers that promote your body to store fat rather than burn fat.

A Doctor's Job

The definition of the word doctor is to teach. As a doctor, I like to think of myself as a golf coach when I help my patients. If you go to the driving range and hit a bucket of balls your game will gradually get better. However, if you had the guidance of a professional golfer who can show you how to properly swing the club and all the other nuances that are involved with playing golf, your game will improve more rapidly. I hope to do the same by teaching you how stress can trigger hormones that promote fat storage and not the breakdown of fat. How foods can trigger hormonal responses that work for you or against you in your weight loss goals. How exercise and the intensity of your workout can trigger the burning of fat or the breakdown of muscle.

Just as the golf pro tweaks your swing, I may adjust your diet and exercise routine. How much of an "adjustment" that needs to be made depends on you. If your results from dieting and exercising are paying off, there may be very little that needs to be adjusted. However, if you're not losing the weight you want, not keeping it off and not getting the muscle tone you want. You need to follow the suggestions you'll find in the book. If you don't make any adjustments, you're going to keep getting the same results. I think the classic definition of insanity is doing the same thing over and over hoping for a different result. Therefore, give the suggestions I make 60-90 days to measure your progress.

With 75% of all doctor visits being stress related, it's obvious to see that it may play a part in your weight loss efforts. Working with many patients, who have a wide variety of health issues, has allowed me the opportunity to witness firsthand the clinical findings that pertain to health and wellness. Initially trained as a chiropractic physician, I learned the body has an innate ability to heal itself. This education gave me a great foundation in biochemistry, physiology and endocrinology, which has given me a great understanding of what happens to the body when we diet, exercise and stress our body. Having a passion for sports all of my life, my professional training also included sports medicine and sports training. I took all that knowledge and combined it with the additional knowledge I received as a clinical nutritionist. Using all these aspects in my practice, I am able to look at the whole patient with all their symptoms and complaints and work to bring them back to good health as well as help them lose weight and shape up their body.

I look at patients from more than one perspective and with more of a **holistic** view to help with their health issues. If their complaint is weight loss, I not only look at their exercise routine as a trainer would, but I also look at the symptoms they complain of and am able to design a plan that treats the cause of their symptoms. This promotes better health and incidentally better fitness begins with better health. It's fairly simple to evaluate and design a workout and diet regimen for someone if you only consider their weight loss goals without taking into account their current health issues. The more challenging part is designing a diet and exercise plan for someone who wants to lose weight but also complains of fatigue, headaches, PMS, menopause, heartburn, indigestion, bloating, gas, constipation, irritability, mood swings, low blood sugar, arthritis, diabetes, allergies and other symptoms. I truly think you need to take those symptoms into consideration when you design a diet and exercise plan for someone, because I don't remember ever seeing a patient who only complained of weight gain without any other type of symptom.

Every person is different. We all have different complaints and different goals. The common goal that we all have who are reading this book is to help figure out how to lose weight and keep it off. I plan on showing you how stress, diet and exercise triggers your hormones to burn or store fat. The one thing I hope you can remember is that each person who reads this book will have a different set of health issues, complaints and symptoms. Although we all want to lose weight and keep it off. If you don't include those different health issues (symptoms) into your weight loss plan, that could be slowing down your results. *The mistake is assuming all those health issues, complaints and symptoms your body gives you has no effect on the success of your weight loss efforts.*

I made it a point to explain all the complicated biochemistry and physiology in easy layman's terms, so you can get a better understanding of how your body functions and how to make it work in your favor. I pray you enjoy the book.

Chapter One

Good Health and Good Fitness

Imagine for a moment you are lost in the mountains one night with no supplies and you're only dependent upon yourself for survival. As you search for the right direction to return home safely, you come upon an empty cabin to take shelter in. There is a huge fireplace inside and you realize the importance of getting a fire started to keep warm through the night. As you search the cabin you joyfully find some matches and three stacks of wood in front of the fireplace. One of the stacks consists of small twigs, another stack is made up of small branches and the third stack, which is the largest, consists of large pieces of chopped wood.

Your goal should be to get a fire started, keep it burning all night and have it burn hot enough to keep you warm. With that in mind, which of the three stacks of wood do you want to burn? It's obvious you need the twigs and small branches to get the fire started, but it will be the big logs, that will generate the most heat and burn for the longest period of time.

The human body functions much like that of the fireplace and those different stacks of logs. Think of those stacks of twigs, small branches and logs as carbohydrates, proteins and fats, which are the calories the body burns to produce heat (energy). In the scenario above, we need to have more big logs stacked up and stored, than

1

we do of twigs and small branches. Unfortunately, the growing American public is just like our little cabin in the woods. We have an overabundant supply of big logs (fat) stockpiled on our body. Unlike our scenario, we don't need to have that many big logs (fat) stored away, but there seems to be an endless supply. Stored body fat found on the body is like those big logs. When we get them to burn, they produce more energy (heat) compared to the amount of energy (heat) we get when we burn calories from carbohydrates or proteins.

Which calories are you burning?

Most Americans are constantly fighting to keep that little fireplace of theirs burning. The number one problem and biggest reason why most of us aren't having success in our never ending weight loss battle, is that we are constantly burning more of the twigs and branches as opposed to the huge supply of logs (stored body fat) that are available. Our bodies should constantly be burning those logs (fat) not those twigs and branches!

When you can continually trigger your body to burn more of the logs than the twigs and branches, you will finally succeed with your weight loss goals. The key is to have that little fireplace of ours constantly burning calories, but more importantly, burning more calories from the stored fats as opposed to constantly burning calories from carbohydrates and proteins.

Many people are following some type of diet and/or exercise program without reaching their desired goals of losing weight, keeping it off and toning up. Why is losing weight and keeping it off such a problem for most people?

Perhaps the reason we can't come up with the right answers to this puzzling question is because we're asking all the wrong questions. There is an old saying that says "you don't need to have the right answers if you don't ask the right questions." Could it be more than just eating the right amount of calories? Could it be more than just eating the right amount of fats? Could it be more than just exercising that will have an effect on our weight loss efforts? Are those the right questions? It's obvious the answers we're getting are in many cases not the answers to why we can't seem to successfully lose weight and keep it off. That's why we need to look at some different questions, because if we keep asking the same questions we're going to get the same answers. These are all good questions, but there are some additional considerations we should be making as well.

Some of the questions we need to be asking are:

> **Can stress affect whether or not our body burns or stores fat?**
> **Can stress be affecting our hormones?**
> **Do our hormones have an affect on our body weight and metabolism?**
> **Is the stress in our life affecting the balance of our hormones?**
> **Is our diet disrupting hormonal balance?**
> **Can the foods we eat trigger our body to burn or store body fat?**
> **Does exercise trigger our body to burn**

calories from stored body fat?
Is it important to just burn calories or do we need to
examine where those calories come from?

Most people today only want to concentrate on counting calories, counting fats and keeping track of exercise. In this book we will answer those questions that aren't being asked. This may help many people who have been unsuccessful with their weight loss results, even though they've been dieting and exercising. If you're like most people, you don't want to waste all your time, energy and efforts dieting and working out without getting the results you want.

We also need to address how our hormones are involved because many people are dieting and exercising and not losing weight. Just think about it, if you are unable to lose weight, keep it off and tone-up the body while you are dieting and exercising, what else could it be?

The Purpose of Diet and Exercise

Most people who diet and exercise simply want to look and feel better each day. Many have stated that if they were happy and content with the way they physically looked, they will feel better about themselves. If that's true most people will start feeling better about themselves once they get their body to start looking more physically fit. For some people becoming a little more fit may mean dropping 20-40 pounds. Others may define more fit, as keeping their weight the same but would like to firm up their arms and legs. Still others would be happy if they could keep the weight off for more than a few months.

"To Burn or Not To Burn, Fat is the Question" was written to help people understand that healthy weight loss is not based solely on diet and exercise. Stress can be one of the main contributors to the puzzle! Stress can be triggering many hormonal responses that can work against all our dieting and exercising efforts. My goal is to share with you how constant and excessive stress can cause hormonal imbalance and trigger your body to work against you, despite all your dieting and exercising efforts. How diet and exercise can trigger hormonal responses that make your body store fat and not burn it.

To achieve healthy weight loss, you need to look not only at diet and exercise but also how stress affects weight loss. In particular, we need to pay attention to the hormonal responses that are triggered from stress, diet and exercise. Those hormones determine whether or not we are placing logs in our fireplace or just twigs and small branches. This is why counting calories and fat grams may not be the total answer to our weight loss problems. Just because we have a roaring fire constantly burning in our little cabin, don't assume the source of that fire came from all the big logs we have stockpiled. That roaring fire may be the result of twigs and small braches constantly being burned.

The major underlying theme of this book is to help you become healthier - not just become thinner! There are plenty of skinny unhealthy people walking around today. My goal is to help you maximize the time, energy and effort you spend dieting and exercising, while at the same time promote better health.

The three pieces of the puzzle (stress, diet and exercise), which we will explore are all very important. The first topic we will discuss will be the effects stress has on our hormonal system.

First, hormones help regulate our weight because they trigger the body to burn calories from stored body fat, lean muscle tissue or from the foods recently eaten. When your hormones are out of balance due to stress, you may be fighting a losing battle when it comes to weight loss. Stress plays a key in regulating your hormones. Are you always under lots of stress? Is your life constantly on the go? Are there other health complaints stressing your body?

Do you even know where your stress is coming from? How can you tell if stress is affecting your health? Have you been failing with your weight loss goals even though you have been dieting and exercising? These are all questions you may need to answer in order to succeed in a healthy weight loss program. Maybe all the stress you have been living under has thrown your hormones so out of balance that it has attributed to your inability to lose the extra weight and keep the weight off.

Secondly, we will discuss the effects foods (diet) have on your blood sugar and how they trigger certain hormonal responses. Is what you eat and drink triggering your body to burn calories from stored body fat, lean muscle tissue or from what you just ate a few hours ago? Does your diet throw your hormones further out of balance? Can hormonal imbalances cause your body to burn more calories from carbohydrates and proteins instead of from stored body fat? Which foods are you eating? Are you choosing foods that throw your hormones further out of balance? We will explain how certain foods will either trigger your body to burn more calories from fat while other foods will trigger your body to store all those extra calories. Remember, just because you're burning calories, doesn't mean you're burning calories from fat.

The final part of this book covers exercise and the type of exercise routine to follow if we want to keep burning calories from fat. We will discuss how to maximize your exercise routine in order to firm and tone the body. Are you exercising? Are you over-training? Do your workouts give you the results you want? Do your workouts trigger your body to burn calories from stored body fat or do you just burn calories? Do you train at an intensity level that is too high and counterproductive?

My goal for this book is to look at some of the questions that are not being asked. We have to many Americans who are overweight and not losing weight even though they are cutting calories, fats and doing some type of exercise. Maybe our hormones and the triggering effects they play on our body due to stress, diet and exercise need to be examined. Therefore, if you haven't received the results you wanted from all your time, energy and efforts in trying to lose weight and tone up, this book will help you examine some different questions to this very puzzling issue.

Good Health vs. Good Fitness

Is good health the same as good fitness? Let's spend a moment addressing "good fitness" and "good health." Most people believe if you are in good physical shape then you are in good health. That's not completely accurate! Are you in good physical shape? Are you physically fit? Can you run two miles? Can you do a dozen pushups? Can you hold your breath for a minute? Can you bend over and touch your toes? These are all questions that pertain to good fitness. If you answered "yes" to all of these questions, you probably are physically fit.

When it comes to good health however, you should be asking some different questions such as, how is your cardiovascular system functioning? How is your reproductive, respiratory, nervous and immune system functioning? Do you complain of constant fatigue, headaches, depression and heartburn? Do you suffer from constipation, bloating and gas? These are questions that pertain to good health. If you answered "yes" to some of these questions, I don't think you can say you are experiencing good health.

As you can plainly see, good fitness is quite different than good health. Let's not assume just because someone looks physically fit from the outside that they are also healthy on the inside. Many men and women with beautiful physiques on the outside are plagued with fatigue, headaches, digestive difficulties, arthritis, difficulty sleeping and food cravings on the inside. I believe good fitness begins with good health.

Patient Story

Debra wanted me to help her with some of her aches and pains as she prepared for an upcoming sports competition. Debra was in excellent physical shape on the outside. Her body fat was about 12 percent and she worked out 4-6 times a week with both aerobic and anaerobic training.

As we began evaluating her symptoms, we discovered that she suffered from bloating, gas, constipation, sinusitis, difficulty sleeping, migraine headaches and an inability to stay awake past nine o'clock at night.

Although Debra looks wonderful on the outside, on the inside her body is dealing with various health issues that are hindering her well-being. Therefore, just because someone looks great physically on the outside, don't assume they are also in great health.

Keep in mind, health is not only defined as "absence of disease," but should also be thought of as vigor and vitality for life. In short, "good fitness" does not always equal "good health." I want to share how we can bring these two categories closer together. As we go through this book and follow the actions steps at the end of each chapter, we can bring these two terms closer together.

Hormonal Balance is the Key

It's not just the calories! It's not just the fats! It's not just dependent on what time you eat! Nor is it simply the exercises that you are doing that will determine if your body is going to gain additional weight or not. To achieve long-term and lasting results from your dieting efforts you need to balance your hormones and properly regulate them. If you restore balance back to your body and rebalance your hormonal system, you can return your body back to good health. As you restore your body back into a state of good health, you will find that your body doesn't have to hold on to so much extra body fat. A healthy body doesn't need all the excess body fat. All that extra weight places more stress on our bones, muscles, joints and back. It makes our heart work harder and taxes our cardiovascular system. It affects our breathing, immune system, respiratory and cardiovascular system I can go on and on how this extra weight is taxing your body. As you become healthier, your ability to keep the weight off will increase as you get healthier.

The hormones that need to be in balance are those that are produced by our endocrine system; the adrenal glands, thyroid and pancreas. The thyroid gland regulates our metabolism, which controls the rate at which our body burns calories. However, the hormones produced by the adrenal glands help determine if our body is going to burn calories from stored body fat, lean muscle tissue or foods we recently consumed. Are the hormones that your thyroid and adrenal glands produce being properly regulated? Or are they so far out of balance from stress, fad diets, poor nutrition and lifestyle choices that they are not working for you, but rather against you. These could be some of the simple reasons why you don't succeed in your weight loss efforts.

Two hormones that are produced in the pancreas, which need to be examined are insulin and glucagon. These two hormones are involved in regulating our blood sugar levels, which is very important in controlling your weight. These hormones are triggered in response to what we eat and drink on a daily basis.

Insulin is produced in response to carbohydrates and is considered an anabolic hormone. Anabolic is defined as to build up or to grow. Glucagon, on the other hand, is produced in the absence of carbohydrates and is a catabolic hormone. The definition of catabolic is to breakdown and tear apart. Is your body producing the proper balance of these two hormones to burn fat and keep your blood sugar level? Does your diet cause you to produce more insulin, which can make you heavier? Do you produce enough glucagon to keep your blood sugar level? Can stress effect how these two hormones operate? Do the food choices you make each day drive your blood sugar levels so far out of balance that it makes it more difficult to succeed in a healthy, weight management program?

Lastly, are you getting a good balance of both aerobic and anaerobic training in your schedule? Are you mistakenly doing more of one type of training than the other, which can throw you out of balance? Does one type of training burn more calories from fats than the other? Can the intensity level you train at produce an imbalance of aerobic and anaerobic metabolism? Is your aerobic training triggering aerobic metabolism or is it triggering anaerobic metabolism? Does it matter what type of exercise you do?

These are some the most essential questions we need to be asking if we are going to look at how stress, diet and exercise triggers the body to burn or store fat, which is the most fundamental process we need to do to succeed with any healthy weight loss program. Ask yourself is your stress level, diet (blood sugar level) and exercise routine working in your favor to promote healthy weight loss? Or, does the stress in your life, the food choices you make and the type of workout you perform throw your hormones further out of balance and make your body work against you? If you're not triggering your body to burn calories from stored fat, you will always be struggling with your weight.

Summary

- Hormones have a direct response on which calories the body burns for energy.
- The goal of a good weight loss program is to trigger the break down of calories from fat.
- Stress, diet and exercise trigger various hormonal responses that we have some control over.
- Good fitness is not the same as good health.
- If proper diet and exercise is not promoting weight loss, it may be the stress level in your life that needs some adjusting.

Action Steps

- Finish reading the book and understand the concepts.
- Set a goal for how much weight you would like to lose, what clothes size you want to fit in or what kind of shape you want your body to become.
- Figure out how long it will take you to reach your goal how many months or years, be realistic.
- Write down your goals and look at them every day to remind yourself where you want to be.
- Commit yourself to take the actions needed to make your goal come true.
- Ask a friend or family member to help hold you accountable to your goal.

Chapter Two

Stress and the Adrenal Glands

Let's first discuss stress and how stress affects the body's ability to burn calories from stored body fat. The reason we want to discuss stress is because stress is everywhere and has a direct bearing on our weight loss efforts. We constantly hear how stress affects our health. The more stress we continually place on our body, the weaker the immune system becomes.

Stress and the immune system are inversely related. As the stress in our life increases, our immune system decreases. We've heard the stories of people working long hours, not getting enough sleep, eating poorly etc. These are the ones who very often catch a cold or infection. They over taxed their immune system with stress and

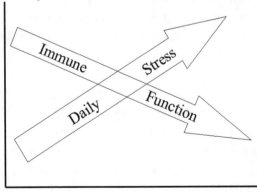

As our stress increases, our immune system decreases.

allowed their body to become susceptible to any invading germ, infection, virus or bacteria.

The immune system keeps you healthy and protects you from infections, diseases and illnesses. Yet, stress and the amount of stress we place upon ourselves can have an effect on how successful we are on any type of weight loss program. In fact, excessive, constant stress will begin to exhaust the function of our adrenal glands, which can hinder any weight loss program.

The adrenal glands sit on top of our kidneys and produce many different hormones that help regulate the body. In fact, if the adrenal glands were removed we would not be able to survive. They are extremely valuable and you never hear of someone having their adrenal glands removed. Most of us may be familiar with the hormone adrenaline and the impact it has on the body. We've heard people speak of an adrenaline rush and that supercharged feeling we get when our body produces extra adrenaline, but there are other hormones produced by our adrenal glands besides adrenaline. Our sex hormones (estrogen, progesterone and testosterone) are also produced by the adrenal glands. The regulation of water, fluids, sodium and potassium are also regulated by the hormones produced by the adrenal glands.

One important feature that is overlooked when examining the function of the adrenal glands is that they help regulate our blood sugar. This can be very important if you are trying to lose weight or if you always feel hungry, light-headed and irritable if your go more than a few hours without eating.

One of the main responsibilities of the adrenal glands is to produce hormones that respond to stress. Many people overlook the effects of stress and the importance it plays with our weight loss efforts. When we're under constant stress, the adrenal glands produce hormones in response to that stress to protect itself from whatever stress may be attacking. When the adrenal glands are constantly responding to stress and are in a state of exhaustion due to constant stress, it can affect the body's ability to break down fats for energy. The most important aspect you need to achieve to succeed in maintaining a healthy weight loss program is getting your body to burn calories from stored body fat. However, when our adrenal glands are exhausted and fatigued due to constant stress, this causes both an over or under production of various hormones that can trigger the body to break down protein (lean muscle tissue) and carbohydrates for energy, not stored body fat.

Knowing that, ask yourself, how is the stress level in your life? Is the stress high enough that it keeps driving your hormones further out of balance? Can the hormonal imbalance caused by the constant stress in your daily life be triggering your body to store more body fat than it can burn?

Many patients complain that their thyroid is under-active and that is the reason they can't lose weight and keep it off. However, it is possible the adrenal glands are exhausted due to constant stress, which is slowing down or impairing the function of the thyroid, which may be why the thyroid is under-active

.

Patient Story

Sue was having difficulty losing weight. She had previously been told her thyroid was the problem and had been taking medication and nutritional supplementation to support her thyroid.

As I was evaluating Sue, she told me that the mental stress in her life is constant and doesn't seem to be getting any better. Many of her symptoms; fatigue, weight gain, poor digestion, constipation, irritability if meals are delayed or missed, mid-afternoon cravings, low blood sugar and the need to eat every 2-3 hours, made me suspect possible adrenal exhaustion.

After identifying some of the things she was doing that were interfering with her health, I implemented a plan that was designed to reduce some of those symptoms and properly support her adrenal glands. Within a few short weeks her list of health complaints were diminishing and she finally started losing those inches that before seemed impossible for her to lose.

The constant stress placed on the adrenal glands can create hormonal imbalance, which could be affecting your thyroid. This sets up a domino effect. The exhausted adrenals can affect the function of the thyroid, which affects how fast we burn calories. This can cause food cravings that can lead to poor choices of food selections that can lead to nutritional deficiencies that could lead to having a weakened immune system, that allows for the susceptibility of infections and illness and so on and so forth. It's like a vicious cycle. One hormone out of balance can trigger a whole host of other reactions and imbalances that may have a negative effect on your body and your health.

Remember, the thyroid regulates the rate the body burns calories in our little fireplace, not so much where those calories are coming from. We burn calories from fats, proteins and carbohydrates. Our goal should be to make sure the body is in a constant state of burning calories from fat, specifically fat stored on the body. However excessive, constant stress will prevent the body from being able to burn calories from fat or stored body fat. The constant daily stress you place on yourself may be what is triggering your body to only burn calories from carbohydrates and proteins and not calories from stored body fat. This is why controlling stress is such an important piece of the puzzle in our efforts to succeed with any healthy weight loss program.

Where Does Stress Come From

We have all heard the expression "the straw that broke the camels back." How does that statement apply to you? For most, it simply means that if you continue to pile more and more stress (straws) on your body each day, that load will become so heavy it will eventually break your camel's back. Ask yourself, what straws are you constantly carrying on your camel's back each day that is causing your camel to work harder? The point is if you reduce some of the straws from your camel's back, he'll be able to carry the load much easier. This is so important because there will be times in your life when you'll have to carry additional straws and if your camel is already overloaded it will break his back. This is how disease and dysfunction begins to tear away at our health.

How many straws are you carrying around each day?

The human body is very similar to the analogy of the camel. If you continue to keep adding more stress onto your body, it will catch up and eventually affect the function of your health unless you learn to limit or reduce the stress in your life. **As stress increases, our immune system decreases.**

The body is capable of responding to huge amounts of stress, however constant stress that lasts for days, weeks, months, years and decades that affects our immune system, eventually wears down the functional capabilities of our adrenal glands.

Think of the adrenal glands as a thoroughbred horse. This horse can run strong and hard when needed. However, this thoroughbred horse also needs to be rested and nourished. How good of a job do you do in resting and nourishing your adrenal glands? Is the stress in your life so high that it is constantly making your horse run hard every day? Are you making your horse carry a heavy load of straws (stress) strapped to his back? Don't you realize if you take some of the weight off his back he'll run better? You cannot expect your horse to run like a champion if you make it run hard every day. That horse needs to be rested and nourished, just like you do. If you want your body to be able to handle all the stress you place on it each day, make sure you are resting and nourishing your body, as well as reducing the amount of stress you place on yourself each day.

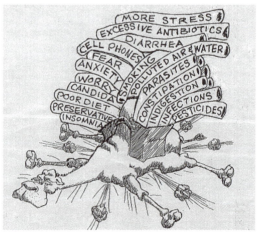

Have you over-stressed your camel?

When patients complain of fatigue, depression, inability to concentrate, weight gain, PMS, irritability, food cravings and other uncomfortable symptoms, I usually begin with a variety of questions such as, how's the stress in your life? Do you complain of bloating, gas or indigestion? How are you nourishing your body? Do you exercise? Are you resting your body? You can't expect your body to operate like a champion, if you keep adding more stress to your life.

Patient Story

Robyn came to my office wondering why she hadn't been able to lose weight even though she claimed to be faithfully following a diet and exercise program. She had gained 35 pounds over the last four years and had tried everything to lose the unwanted weight. She was always on the go from morning until nighttime and said her stress level always seems to be mounting.

After evaluating her list of symptoms which included; fatigue, low blood sugar, mood swings, crave sweets in the afternoon, needs caffeine to keep going throughout the day, lightheadedness, difficulty with her monthly cycle, allergies, two rounds of antibiotics the past year, history of yeast infections, constipation, bloating and gas. She realized that her health was not as good as she thought.

We implemented a plan to repair her digestive system, which ensured better absorption of the nutrients that were specifically targeted for her adrenal glands. Within a couple of weeks she started feeling less fatigue, her food cravings diminished, the bloating and gas were gone and her allergies lessened. After only a months time of nourishing her adrenal glands she lost ten pounds and finally slide below 160 pound, which she hadn't been able to do for two years.

> It was an accumulation of all the different types of stress that was over-taxing her body and triggering all the wrong hormones. Her body was constantly burning calories from carbohydrates and proteins, not stored body fat, due to all the stress that was attacking her body.

As we have covered, the adrenal glands respond to stress and if the adrenals are exhausted, not only will you have a difficult time losing weight, but you may also suffer from fatigue, low blood sugar, food cravings, allergies, PMS, menopause, asthma, depression, high blood pressure, headaches, irritability, mood swings, digestive difficulties, inability to concentrate, anxiety, and difficulty sleeping. If this sounds like you, then you need to do a better job of resting and nourishing your adrenals and look to see where all your stress is coming from.

One of the main functions of the adrenal glands is to produce hormones in response to stress. The over-or-under production of these hormones can be measured to determine the level of stress we are under. This is very useful information to determine the functional capacity of our adrenal glands and our immune function. This may provide the answers to our inability to lose weight, but also why many other health complaints are affecting us.

We will discuss later how to measure adrenal stress, but let's first review the different types of stress. Most people believe there is only one type of stress, mental and emotional stress that affects our health. Unfortunately, there are several other forms of stress that we need to be aware of.

Types of Stress

Mental / Emotional Stress - worry, anger, frustration, fear, depression

Physical Stress - too much exercise, not enough exercise, inadequate or poor sleep, injuries, accidents, trauma, aches and pains, surgery.

Chemical - prescription drugs, over-the-counter medications, pesticides and insecticides in our food, antibiotics, processed and refined foods, artificial sweeteners, colors, flavors and preservatives, toxic or heavy metal exposure, polluted air and water.

Internal pollution - constipation, diarrhea, indigestion, heartburn, bloating, gas, acid reflux, food allergies.

Microbial toxicity - overgrowth of candida, yeast, fungus and parasites.

Nutritional Deficiencies - inadequate supply of vitamins, minerals, antioxidants, essential fatty acids, enzymes, and fiber.

Electro-magnetic - constant exposure to electrical devices such as computers, televisions, cell phones, microwaves, fluorescent lights, electric blankets, waterbeds, pagers, hair dryers and clock radios. (insert photo of EMF)

How much electro-magnetic stress are you exposed to each day?

The IRS Approach to Health

I = **Identify & Implement**
R = **Remove & Repair**
S = **Support & Strengthen**

As you can see there are many different types of stress that affect our health that we often times don't think about. The IRS Approach is a step-by-step process and an acronym that is used to help each person know where they are as they work to restore their health. The more you tax your body with different types of stress the harder your immune system has to work, the larger the tax, the greater the burden. Are you over-taxing your body? Are you making your adrenal glands have to work harder? If you are this could have a big effect on your body's ability to burn calories from fat.

Look at the different types of stresses in your life you may realize that you may be placing to many straws on your camel's back, which may be the cause for your inability to lose weight. As I said earlier, you cannot only look at someone's desired weight loss goals and design a plan without taking into consideration all the different symptoms that are affecting their health. All those symptoms are communicating something to us, whether we want to take the time and listen to what our body is trying to say, is the question that needs to be answered. Our body is letting us know that something isn't working right, and there's some imbalance, which is causing all those symptoms.

If your goal is to successfully lose weight and keep it off it is important to first get healthy. The IRS Approach is designed to restore health, which will improve our weight loss results. The first part of the IRS Approach is to **Identify** all the different stresses that are taxing your body and interfering with your bodies natural innate ability to heal itself, then **Implement** a plan that can be followed that will begin to restore health.

The second phase is to **Remove** any toxins, microbes and any other interfering factors that are stressing your body. Once that has been completed you can begin to **Repair** any damage that has been caused by the additional stress.

The final part of the IRS Approach is meant to **Support and Strengthen** the body. It surprises me how many patients are taking 20, 30, even 40 bottles of different supplements and are not feeling great. I'm a big believer that repairing someone's health is like painting a house. A good painter knows that before you start slapping paint on those walls, it's smart to prep those walls in order for the paint to stick.

The human body is very similar. There are so many patients who complain of heartburn, bloating, gas, indigestion, food allergies, yeast, candida, parasites, constipation and diarrhea that it effects their ability to absorb nutrients from their food. These people definitely need to Repair their gastrointestinal system (GI tract) first, in order to promote better absorption of their nutrients otherwise they may not be getting much value from their supplements. It is often stated, "You are what you eat," I think it is more accurate to say, "you are what your body absorbs." Just because you ate it don't think that you automatically absorbed it.

When you following the IRS Approach to health, the goal is to lighten the load from all the different stresses that can be over-taxing your body. As you do this you will begin to notice the changes in your health and realize that good fitness begins with good health.

Take a look at all the different types of **mental, emotional stresses** that affect your health and your quality of life. If those stresses are high, you need to take some action and lower those stresses. There are many different ways to help you control emotional and mental stress. Whether it is the guidance of a professional counselor, prayer, meditation, biofeedback, hypnosis or visualization something needs to be done to lower this tax to your body. The simplest and least expensive remedy you can do to help yourself is to breath. Slow, deep breathing for a few minutes can disrupt the negative effects of cortisol. If you only take 5 minutes a day to close your eyes and relax for a moment with some deep breathing, you can lower the output of cortisol, which is usually very high when you are stressed.

We all know that fear, anger and worry attribute to mental stress, but did you know that physical exercise can be stressful? Are you over-training? Do you get enough sleep, enough water? Do you have constant aches and pains, which are physically demanding on the body? Review the physical stress your applying to your body and make the necessary adjustment to lower that stress.

Have you thought about all the different chemicals you put in your body? Drugs and over-the-counter medications can tax our liver, kidneys, and stomach and affect their functional capabilities. How do the toxins in the water and air affect us? How do all the preservatives, artificial sweeteners, flavors and ingredients affect our body. How does refined, processed foods affect our system. How do insecticides and pesticides found in our food affect our health? These are some of the chemical stresses we place on our body each day so much so that many people fail to think about them when they start wondering why they have a particular health issue. **A good cleansing and detoxification program to remove many of the toxins that buildup in the liver, intestines, kidneys, and lymphatic system can reduce the toxic burden on the body.**

Internal stress is something that is often overlooked. When your body is dealing with constipation, diarrhea, bloating, gas, heartburn, food allergies it is more stressful and taxing to the body. The internal poisoning from constipation is taxing to the body. The environment your tissues and cells live in can be very toxic. I know I don't want to live in an area where the air pollution is bad so why do I want to have all my tissues and cells living in a polluted internal environment? It's very taxing! There's a tax to pay for all the bloating, gas, indigestion and reflux we expose our body to. Remember all those antacids and other medications for bloating, gas, indigestion and reflux are only band-aiding the symptom. They are not treating the cause. **Digestive enzymes, hydrochloric acid and proper food combining can help relieve this stress.**

Microbial toxicity is another overlooked stressor. Candida, yeast overgrowth and parasites tax our body. A weakened immune system allows the exacerbation of these problems. One reason why intestinal health is so vital is that over 50% of our immune system is found in the digestive system. Internal poisoning can contribute to these problems. Good intestinal bacteria keeps the proliferation of candida and yeast over-growth to a minimum but the use of birth control pills, antibiotics and steroid hormones will contribute to candida over-growth. Traveling to a third world country is not the only way to become infected with parasites. Raw foods, pork, sushi and contaminated food and water contribute to the problem. **Good intestinal bacteria referred to as probiotics, such as lactobacillus acidophilus and bifodobacterium bifidum, along with a candida and parasite cleanse can help reduce this stress.**

Nutritional deficiencies can be a major stress. We can't expect our body to function well if we don't give it enough water. How do we expect our body to function properly if we don't give the body enough vitamins, mineral, antioxidants, essential fatty acids and fiber which are the some of the raw materials needed to produce hormones, antibodies, enzymes and neurotransmitters (brain messengers)? Our body doesn't magically manufacture these things, nor do we have an endless supply that can be manufactured. If your body is nutritionally deficient, that is another tax on the body. **A multivitamin/ mineral supplement with antioxidants and essential fatty acids will help support and strengthen our immune system.**

Electro-magnetic stress is a newer way of taxing our body, which we are only starting to learn about. Computers, cell phones, pagers, televisions, microwaves and other electrical appliances emit an electro-magnetic field. Our nervous system also uses electrical impulses to send information to every muscle, organ and tissue of the body. It is possible that the electrical magnetic fields coming from these electrical units are interfering with the electrical impulses our nervous system is transmitting. This could be a reason for some of our health problems. The earth has a magnetic pull, which is why compasses work. However, when you are inside a building or home with three feet of concrete, insulated walls and you are bombarded with electro-magnetic energy from computers, cell phones, beepers, microwaves, electrical appliances, televisions, radios, fluorescent light etc., this may interfere with that compass and the way the nervous system tries to communicate to its organs, muscles and tissues. **Carrying a bipolar magnet with you during the day as you work around these electro magnetic fields can help alleviate this tax to your body.**

As you can see, there are other types of stress besides mental and emotional stress we need to be concerned with. Evaluate each of these categories and identify which of the other types of stress you are burdening your body with. You may find that your emotional stress is in control but you are overtaxing yourself with excessive internal, microbial and electro-magnetic stress! Or quite possibly, excessive physical and chemical stress along with nutritional deficiencies could be the root cause of your unexplained symptoms or health issues. Does your diet adequately supply nutrients in order to support the function of your adrenals, thyroid, liver, kidneys, brain, heart, etc.? Are you constantly exposing your body to electro-magnetic stress? Are you adding more physical stress to the ledger by working out too hard or too long? If you neglect to recognize some of the other types of stress besides mental stress that can be affecting your health, you may find yourself continually fighting a never-ending battle with a particular health issue. This is why just like in war, if you don't know who your enemies are, how do you know who to protect yourself from?

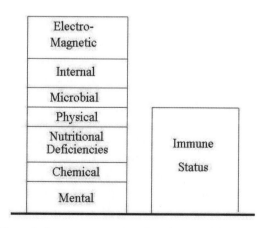

Cumulative stress greater than immune function.
Highly susceptible to diseases and infections.

Electro-Magnetic	
Internal	Immune
Microbial	
Physical	Status
Nutritional Deficiencies	
Chemical	
Mental	

Immune function greater than cumulative stress.
Highly resistant to diseases and infections.

Whatever type of stress is taxing your body, it is important to realize stress has a cumulative effect on our health. Just like the straws on a camel's back, we need to make sure that we are not overtaxing our body with excessive stress, as this weakens our immune system and causes our adrenal glands to work harder. If you keep making your adrenal glands work hard everyday because of excessive, constant stress, you eventually exhaust their functional capabilities.

Remember, my underlying goal for this book is to get you healthier while helping you lose weight and keep it off. Identifying where the stress in your life is coming from is the first step needed to promote good health and restore your adrenal glands to proper function. You will see, as you get healthier, the body doesn't need to carry around all that unhealthy and unwanted extra layer of fat.

The following is a list of some of the symptoms that are associated with adrenal exhaustion. You may find some of the symptoms that have plagued you could be associated with adrenal exhaustion. This is why it is so important to look at all the different forms of stress that can be overtaxing your body.

Symptoms Associated
with Adrenal Exhaustion

- Weight gain or inability to lose weight
- Fatigue & weakness
- Crave sweets or coffee
- Low blood sugar problems
- Irritable before meals or if meals are delayed
- Shaky or lightheaded if meals are delayed
- Depression, mood swings, irritability
- Difficulty building muscle
- Increased susceptibility to colds, flu' and infections
- Difficulty Sleeping or Insomnia
- Inability to concentrate
- Premenstrual tension
- Indigestion and poor absorption
- Low body temperature
- Can't fall back to sleep at night
- Reduced immune function
- Poor memory
- Nervousness
- Unexplained hair loss
- Headaches
- Dizziness that occurs after standing
- Anxiety and restlessness
- Palpitations or heart fluttering
- Food or airborne allergies

  Do any of these sound familiar or are common symptoms for you? After looking at some of the symptoms associated with adrenal exhaustion, it is important to understand how our adrenals deal with stress.

Summary

- As stress increase, immune function decreases.
- The adrenal glands respond to stress.
- Constant stress can exhaust the adrenal glands.
- Stress can show up as various symptoms.
- Excessive stress can prevent the break down of fats.
- There are different types of stress that affect the body.
  - Mental/emotional stress
  - Physical stress
  - Chemical stress
  - Internal stress
  - Microbial stress
  - Nutritional Deficiencies
  - Electro Magnetic Fields

Action Steps

- Evaluate the different types of stress effecting your health.
- Reduce the stress from each one of the different categories.
- Seek help and advise if you're not sure how to control or manage the stress.

Chapter Three

Stressed About Weight Loss

If you had only thought stress came in the form of mental or emotional stress, the last chapter may have surprised a lot of people. When you think about all the different types of stress that affect your body is it any surprise to find out that about seventy-five percent of all doctor visits are stress related. What we want to talk about now is, how the body deals with stress. What effect does stress have on your ability to burn calories from fat?

Fight or Flight versus Resting Digesting

Are you always running from a saber tooth tiger?

31

To better understand what happens to our hormones when we are under stress, we first need to know there are two different systems that constantly regulate our body. The first system is called the Sympathetic or Fight or Flight Mode. The other is called the Parasympathetic or Resting/Digesting Mode. They are part of the Autonomic Nervous System, which regulates the activities of our breathing, heart rate, blood flow, production of hormones, enzymes and the activity of our organs. They accomplish this task 24 hours a day, 7 days a week automatically, without us ever having to concern ourselves with this process. These two systems can be thought of as opposites, meaning one system turns on or initiates a certain response, while the other system turns that response off or causes the opposite action.

The best way to describe how the adrenal glands respond to stress is the story of coming face to face with the "proverbial" saber tooth tiger. There is one of two choices, either run or fight. Neither choice is good, but that is beside the point. The body begins to produce various stress hormones (cortisol, adrenaline and noradrenaline) to protect itself. These hormones are produced in response to stress, which triggers the beginning of the Fight or Flight mode. Now, you either run or fight to protect yourself and it is that adrenaline rush that makes you stronger and faster to deal with this situation.

A simple explanation of what happens when the Fight or Flight mode is active, is that the body directs more blood to your muscles so you will be strong enough to run away or fight the tiger. The heart rate increases in order to push more blood and oxygen to the muscles. The lungs expand so breathing becomes easier; the pupils dilate so peripheral vision is increased. Blood will be directed away from the digestive system, since you don't need to worry about digesting your meal if you're running from a saber tooth tiger. Once you are out of danger and the stress decreases, the Fight or Flight mode will turn off and the Resting/Digesting mode takes over.

When the body is in the Resting/Digesting mode, the heart doesn't beat as fast, breathing is slower and deeper, pupils don't open as large and blood doesn't need to be in all your muscles. Now the energy can be directed to your digestive system and assist in the process of digesting your food and letting your body recover and repair.

If only everyday was like this.

The two systems work in almost direct opposition to one another. When the stress level is high, the Fight or Flight mode turns on several different mechanisms to deal with the stress. Once that stress has been reduced and the body doesn't have to pump all that blood to our muscles, our heart rate decreases, our lungs don't need to expand so large nor do our pupils need to dilate. The Resting/Digesting mode will turn off all those switches. When one system is operating, the other one isn't.

In a typical day, you should spend most of your time in the Resting/Digesting mode and a short amount of time in The Fight or Flight mode. It's impossible to run or "fight that tiger" all day long. Unfortunately, many of us do not keep the proper balance of these two systems and spend more time in the Fight or Flight mode. Although we have no conscious control of the different hormonal responses each system triggers, we can control which systems we spend most of our day in. Are we constantly in the Fight or Flight mode throughout the day? Are we truly in the Resting/Digesting Mode when we eat and rest? Some people don't know what it is to rest and relax. They are constantly on the go. We need to ask these questions because *when the body is under constant, continual stress, certain stress hormones are produced that promote the breakdown of carbohydrates and protein (muscle), while inhibiting the breakdown of fats.*

Today we don't have to worry about saber tooth tigers but many of us are constantly being chased by the proverbial "paper tigers." They don't get enough sleep, they rush to work in the morning, have a quick breakfast (if at all), hurry to get the kids to school, rush to the office, fight traffic, deadlines, meetings, office politics, quick lunches, road rage, pick up the kids, soccer practice, make dinner, homework, take care of the house, spend time with the spouse, bedtime...then start all over again tomorrow.

If this sounds like some part of your day, there is a good chance you are constantly in the Fight or Flight Mode, which is causing your body to produce more of the stress hormones to protect itself. The body always feels like it is under attack. We should spend more of our day in the Resting/Digesting Mode. Whether you realize it or not, you're creating hormonal imbalance that will eventually deplete and exhaust the functional capacity of your adrenal glands and their ability to properly respond to stress. A domino effect of dysfunction begins and unexplained symptoms develop that can hinder your health and vitality. This is why it's important to examine the different types of stress that affect your life and adjust your lifestyle, so that you are not constantly in this Fight or

Flight Mode. If you are living a life under constant stress, this could explain why you have been unable to lose weight, keep it off and add muscle to your body.

The Three Stages of Adrenal Stress

The adrenal glands don't exhaust overnight. It takes time and abuse for this to happen. It was the brilliant researcher, Hans Selye, who first identified the effect stress has on the adrenal glands and their ability to function properly. He coined the term General Adaptive Syndrome and found there are three stages the adrenal glands go through in response to stress.

The first is called the Alarm Stage. This is what happens to the body when we see the saber tooth tiger; heart rate increases, pupils dilate, breathing increases, blood is transported to the muscles and shunted away from the digestive system. All of these activities are turned on and are controlled by the Fight or Flight Mode. Once we get out of danger and the stress decreases, the Resting Digesting Mode will turn off all those body functions that were called into action. The adrenal glands will not have to produce all those stress hormones once we are out of harms way.

It is in Stage Two and Stage Three that all the problems begin. Stage Two is called the Resistance or Adaptive Stage. This is when the stress is continually constant in your life and the body responds by producing large amounts of the various stress hormones to pro-tect itself. It's like asking the military to be at the highest level of alert. The body is trying to adapt to this stressful situation. The question is how long can your adrenals be expected to produce all these hormones before exhaustion and depletion set in? How long before you break your camel's back and symptoms of ill health begins?

The difficulty lies in the fact that you can only be at that constant state of readiness for so long before fatigue and exhaustion sets in.

That's why stage three is called the Exhaustive Stage. The body is still under attack from all the stress. The only difference is that because it has been at such a high state of alert for a long period of time, the body is exhausted and unable to adequately defend itself from an attack. The prolonged stress has finally caught up. The body is unable to respond due to the constant stress. The adrenal glands have been exhausted and are simply worn out and incapable of producing the necessary stress hormones. When this occurs, dysfunction and ill health begins.

Stage three, Functional Adrenal Exhaustion, can be likened to the boxer who enters the final round of the fight and needs to keep fighting but is so fatigued and tired he doesn't have the energy or strength to keep his arms up to fight. That's what functional adrenal exhaustion is like. We want to be able to get up and go throughout the day, after work, on weekends but we just don't have enough energy to keep up. How many people feel this way? Many people wonder why they are constantly exhausted, tired, fatigued, complaining of food craving, low blood sugar, PMS and depression! One common thread of similarity I find with those people who have many of the above stated complaints is that they are suffering from functional adrenal exhaustion.

How this applies to weight lose is profound because when you are under continual stress, the body produces a stress hormone called cortisol. Cortisol is very important for maintaining good health, but cortisol triggers the breakdown of protein, not fat. Therefore, if you are under a great deal of stress for long periods of time and you are not getting the results you expect from all your dieting and exercise efforts, you should see how your body is responding to stress. Are your adrenal glands being triggered to produce a large amount of cortisol in response to stress? Remember there are many different types of stress we need to be aware of. A simple saliva test is a way to measure cortisol levels, which we will discuss later.

When the stress in your life is constantly on the rise or high, this eventually exhausts and affects the functional capabilities of your adrenal glands. This is referred as "hypoadrenia." The word "hypo" means low, in this case the low functioning status of the adrenal glands. *If you suffer from hypoadrenia or low function-ing adrenal glands, this could explain why you have a difficult time losing weight, adding muscle tone and are always fatigued! Why you are constantly fighting infections and allergies! Why PMS cycles and menopause are difficult! Why you complain of food cravings, low blood sugar and digestive problems! Why you have mid-afternoon slumps, feel irritable, moody and depressed! Why you have difficulty sleeping and concentrat-ing!*

As we said before, we can't keep running from that tiger all day. The adrenal glands are very involved with all these issues and have a domino effect on our health and immune system. If your adrenal glands are exhausted and overtaxed, so is your immune system. When the immune system is down you become susceptible to all kinds of diseases, infections and illnesses. This is why it is so important to manage all the different types of stress in your life and properly nourish and rest your adrenal glands. Don't expect your champion racehorse to win any races for you when you keep strap-ping all that extra weight (stress) on his back day after day. Remember, *good fitness begins with good health.*

Many patients, due to our fast, hurry-up society are in stage two and stage three of adrenal exhaustion. Those who are suffering and not getting better from many of today's' health complaints such as fatigue, obesity, food cravings, low blood sugar, depression, PMS, menopause, insomnia, mood swings, irritability, as well as some of the other degenerative and auto immune diseases, should investi-gate how well they are controlling the stress in their life. Are you adequately nourishing your adrenal glands for the amount of stress you are placing them under? Have you placed too much stress on your adrenal glands for too long? Are you suffering from hypoa-drenia or functional adrenal exhaustion?

Functional Adrenal Exhaustion

Now let's explore what happens when the adrenal glands are in stage two (resistance) or stage three (exhaustion). When the body is under stress, a hormone called cortisol is produced. The benefits from cortisol are immense. Cortisol works as an anti-inflammatory and helps with the reduction of pain, swelling and allergic responses. Athletes receive shots of cortisone to help reduce pain or inflammation. Doctors recommend cortisone to help reduce itching and allergies. Cortisol is a beneficial hormone and is involved in many bodily functions.

When you are in stage two of functional hypoadrenia your body is making more cortisol due to the constant stress. The effects of cortisol are quite simple. It promotes the breakdown of protein (lean muscle tissue) and carbohydrates, which is the last thing we want in any weight loss program. Instead we want to be burning calories from fat. However, the excessive production of cortisol inhibits the breakdown of fat. Therefore, if your body is constantly making more cortisol throughout the day in response to stress, you will have a more difficult time burning body fat and building muscle.

I did not say you would not be able to lose weight! An important issue to understand is that even if you lose weight, you may not necessarily lose body fat. Remember cortisol promotes the break down of protein (lean muscle tissue). Did the weight you lost come from stored body fat or did you lose lean muscle tissue? Sure, you may have lost 20 pounds in 30 days, but was it body fat? This is one reason I don't like to only use the scale to determine the effectiveness of a weight loss program. I encourage people to use their mirror and see how their clothes are fitting. Too often patients complain of losing weight but they are not getting any firmer. Typically, they burn lean muscle tissue, which is why their scale shows they lost weight but their percentage of body fat remains the same. The goal is to trigger the body to burn stored body fat.

Another effect of constant cortisol production is that it can increase the production of acids or decrease the sensitivity to acids in the digestive system. This can lead to ulcers and other digestive difficulties like heartburn, indigestion, bloating and gas. Excessive cortisol will decrease the production of white blood cells and cause shrinking of our lymph nodes, which causes a decline in our immune system and allows us to become more susceptible to infections, diseases and illnesses. Excessive cortisol can promote high blood pressure and other vascular disorders.

Stage three of functional hypoadrenia is when the body can't keep up with the demands that are being placed on it. As we said earlier you can only go so long with this high level of alert before you deplete and exhaust the functional capacity of the adrenal glands. When this happens, the body can't even make enough cortisol, which is essential for preservation and we become even more susceptible to other health conditions.

I hope you understand why it is important to examine the different types of stress in your life and see how that can affect your weight loss goals and your overall health. This is why I emphasize getting the body healthier, not just thinner.

Which Hormones to Use

We've been speaking about controlling all the different types of stress, hormonal balance and how stress can cause an over-or-under production of cortisol. Since the adrenal glands are involved with the production of estrogen, progesterone, testosterone and DHEA (dehydroepiandrosterone) it's important to see if we are abusing our adrenal glands and the balance of these hormones. Typically these hormone imbalances are caused by some of the lifestyle choices we make.

Many people have referred to DHEA as the "anti-aging" hormone. DHEA is known to help reduce body fat, increase lean muscle mass, alleviate depression, strengthen the immune system, increase energy, balance blood sugar, reduce joint pain, promote mental clarity, revitalize our sex lives and the list goes on. The benefits of the production of DHEA are profound for the body. As we age the production of DHEA decreases, which may explain why it is called the anti-aging hormone.

The adrenal glands are responsible for the production of both of these two hormones (cortisol and DHEA). Cholesterol is the raw material that is used to build these hormones; in fact, they are on the same assembly line until they meet at the fork in the road. That fork in the road is where stress begins. If there is a high amount of stress in your life, the body will direct that assembly line to produce cortisol in order to protect itself. However, if the stress is controlled or reduced and you do not need so much cortisol, that assembly line can be directed to produce DHEA, which converts into estrogen and testosterone. Therefore, controlling the stress in your life will allow certain hormones (DHEA) to be activated that have a positive impact on your health. If the stress in constant in your life, you may be constantly forcing your body to continually produce cortisol, which means you have less DHEA available.

Ladies, its important to realize that if you had a hysterectomy or are menopausal your ovaries are no longer producing estrogen, proges-terone or testosterone. The adrenal glands will then be solely responsi-ble for the production of these hormones. However, if the adrenal glands are depleted and exhausted how do you expect your body to make these hormones? More importantly, if you complain of low sex drive or lack of "libido" it's probably due to the low production of testos-terone. This can occur if that assembly line is constantly being directed to produce cortisol, which reduces or inhibits the production of DHEA, testosterone, and estrogen. This does not mean go out and start taking testosterone to boost your sex life. Rather, start by treating the cause and begin to reduce all the stress in your life and properly nourish your adre-nal glands in order for them to produce their own testosterone.

Patient Story

Mindy came to my office at the urging of her husband to seek advice for hormonal irregularities and premenstrual syn-drome. She complained of always feeling irritable, with huge mood swings and difficult periods that lasted more than seven days. She wasn't able to lose weight even though she followed a regular workout routine. Her job was demanding and stressful, as was keeping up with three teenagers.

She had overwhelmed herself with so much stress that her body was unable to make the necessary hormones to keep up with her busy life. After reviewing her whole history, one of the suggestions I gave her was to begin using progesterone cream topically. She immediately noticed changes. Her energy level improved, her mood stabilized, her periods became more regular with less cramping.

Being under so much stress, her body was using all that progesterone to make cortisol, which probably didn't leave enough progesterone to produce the other hormones and to keep them in balance. As she supported her body with additional progesterone her body was better able to make these other hormones, which helped alleviate many of her symptoms.

Measuring Adrenal Exhaustion

There are a couple of simple tests that can be done at home to measure the functional status of the adrenal glands. The first is to take your blood pressure lying down then immediately take it standing. What should happen is that the systolic (top) number should increase 6-10 points. If it stays the same or falls that is a good indicator that the adrenals may not be functioning as well as they could be. They're not broke but they're just not doing the job. That is why it is referred to as the functional hypoadrenia.

Many health professionals assume the adrenals are either broke or they are perfectly fine. I believe there is a "gray area" where they aren't functioning like they should. It's like having two cars traveling from point A to point B. They can both get you there, but one is leaking

The ride's just not the same in both cars.

oil, overheating and backfiring. You can't assume because they both carried you there, they are both working the same.

A second simple test to determine the functional status of the adrenal glands is to take a penlight and shine it into someone's eye. A normal response is the pupil will constrict and become smaller from the bright light. If the pupil cannot stay constricted and looks as if it is pulsating, this is another signal the adrenal glands may need some attention.

A hormonal saliva test is one of the best ways to measure the functional status of the adrenal glands. I recommend a hormonal saliva test to many of my patients who not only have a difficult time with weight loss and fatigue, but also to those patients who may be suffering from various health conditions that don't seem to get any better. The hormonal saliva test will measure the production of cortisol and DHEA, which can readily determine the balance of these two hormones and reflect how stress is affecting your health. A saliva test is a better indicator for the functional status of the adrenal glands, because the saliva test is done with four measurements throughout the day as opposed to one measurement that is usually done with a blood analysis. The reason we want to measure the cortisol status for the whole day is that in a 24-hour period the cortisol levels fluctuate. A one-time blood draw won't be able to give as much good information as a 24- hour saliva test would. In addition, the saliva test can be done at home, which eliminates the stress and anxiety of going to the doctor's office, which can cause an abnormal rise in cortisol levels.

If you think your adrenals could be the reason for your lack of success with your weight loss efforts and you have answered yes to many of the questions in the symptom associated with hypoadrenia, I would seriously examine all the different types of stress that could be affecting your life and begin managing them. Stress could be the major culprit to your weight loss problems and could be triggering your hormones to constantly burn carbohydrates and proteins for energy and not fat. It's not just burning calories that is important, but it's burning calories from stored body fat that will finally give us the results we want from our weight loss efforts.

Where does energy come from?

For weight loss and dieting purposes, limiting stress and the production of cortisol is crucial. With excessive amounts of cortisol being produced, the liver is unable to break down fats and instead breaks down carbohydrates (sugars) and proteins (lean muscle) for energy. The break down of fats is the most efficient way for the body to produce energy. In fact, one gram of fat will produce more than two and a half times more energy than a gram of carbohydrate or protein.

To achieve long-term benefits of a healthy weight loss program, it is essential to trigger those hormones that are responsible for the break down of fats. When you're always triggering the break down of carbohydrates (sugar) it's easier to use up all the sugar in your body. This can explain why 2-3 hours after a meal you're complaining of low blood sugar, cravings, fatigue, irritability etc. Our body was only burning calories from carbohydrates (sugars).

Supporting the Adrenal Glands

When I started this book, I said "you don't need the right answer if you don't ask the right questions." Therefore, the difficulty you have been having with your weight loss efforts may have only a small amount to do with your diet and exercise program, but rather a great deal to do with your hormones (adrenals) being out of balance due to stress.

One of the biggest assumptions people make each day is that the body has an endless supply of hormones, enzymes, antibodies and neurotransmitters (brain messengers). People simply assume the body has an endless supply of these. I want to remind you, these hormones, enzymes, antibodies and neurotransmitters that the body manufactures are end products. Our organs and glands make these essential end products, but in order to manufacture any end product we first need to start with raw materials. These raw materials (vitamins, minerals, fatty acids, antioxidants) help keep the assembly line going. Ask yourself, are you giving your body all the raw materials it needs to be healthy or do you feed it junk food and fast food that has no nutritional value? If you're not nourishing your body with enough good nutrients under normal stress conditions, how do you expect to keep them running properly under stressful conditions?

Science has taught us the functions of the hormones produced by the adrenal glands are far reaching. That is why it is so important that the hormones produced by the adrenal glands be at the appropriate levels to maintain good health. Some of the nutrients that are known to support and nourish the adrenal glands are Vitamin C, the B-vitamins, especially vitamin B-5 pantothenic acid, zinc, magnesium, licorice root, ginseng and adrenal glandulars. There should be a small amount of these nutrients found in most of your multivitamins, which should be a staple in everyone's diet. If the levels of the nutrients needed to support the adrenal glands are already low, due to constant stress and neglect, you need to further increase the nutrients that are specifically known to support the adrenals. There are some nutrition manufactures that are aware of the effects of hypoadrenia and market specific products that are designed to specifically nourish the adrenal glands. These are a good start to help you begin nourishing your adrenal glands.

The hormones DHEA and pregnenolone are two supplements that are highly effective in supporting the function of the adrenal glands. However, I would not recommend taking DHEA without first taking a simple hormonal saliva screen to measure your cortisol and DHEA levels. The reason is if you suspect that your DHEA level is low and begin to supplement your diet with DHEA, when in actuality your hormones levels are normal, then you would be contributing to hormonal imbalance and possibly exacerbating health complaints

If you properly nourish your adrenal glands and decrease the excessive stress in your life, your body will do a better job of keeping those hormones in balance. These hormones will then have a triggering effect on your body's ability to burn fat and not store fat, along with your body's ability to control and regulate many of the other symptoms associated with adrenal exhaustion or imbalance.

Summary

- You can't run from the saber tooth tiger all day.
- If your always struggling with excessive stress in your life it could be hampering your weight loss results.
- Let your body rest, recuperate and repair.
- Stress triggers the production of cortisol.
- Cortisol breaks down protein (lean muscle tissue) and inhibits the break down of fat.
- Deep breathing and relaxation can lower cortisol production.

Action Steps

- If you're not having success with your weight loss efforts and you feel that your adrenal glands may be exhausted, begin to rest and nourish them.
- Have your cortisol and DHEA levels checked with a 24-hour saliva test.
- Continue to work at lowering the stress in your life.

Chapter Four

Is the Thyroid to Blame?

At the start of this book I spoke of a little fireplace we all have burning inside. If you can imagine, our thyroid gland functions much like that fireplace and it's responsible for keeping the cabin (body) warm.

The thyroid gland, the adrenal glands, the pancreas and our reproductive organs (ovaries and testes) are merely instruments in the orchestra we call our endocrine system. They are just players in the band, but if one instrument is off key and playing poorly that could disrupt the beautiful sound we expect to hear.

It is common for most people and doctors to suspect the thyroid as the chief problem when weight loss efforts fail, especially when we think our diet and workouts are being followed correctly. What we want to discuss now is the function of the thyroid and its involvement in a good weight loss program.

We just finished learning how stress affects the hormones produced by the adrenal glands and how they can affect our weight loss results. Keep in mind that one hormonal imbalance can trigger another hormonal imbalance. Maybe the function of the thyroid is being affected by the function of the adrenal glands? Maybe the stress in our life is causing a domino effect on our thyroid?

Metabolism

One of the primary functions of the thyroid is to regulate our metabolism, which is defined as the rate at which the body burns calories. Many people complain of having a low thyroid or slow metabolism. The importance of burning calories from stored body fat is the focus of a healthy weight loss plan. We can be burning hundreds of calories daily, but if those calories are coming from the breakdown of protein (lean muscle tissue) and carbohydrates rather than fats, then this could explain why we may not be reaching our weight loss goals. The thyroid may be functioning fine in burning calories. It doesn't determine the source from where those calories come from. We want to make sure we are burning as many logs (fats) as we can.

How hot do you keep your fireplace burning?

Think of the thyroid as a small fireplace responsible for keeping the whole cabin warm. If you place enough logs in that fireplace, it should generate enough heat to warm the whole cabin. However, if you don't place enough logs in the fireplace, you only heat up the area closest to the fireplace and do not generate enough heat to warm the furthest corners of the room. Do you complain of always having cold hands and feet? Maybe your fireplace (thyroid) isn't burning enough logs (calories) to keep the whole room warm. This could be a thyroid problem.

What is a calorie?

A calorie is nothing more than a unit of measurement of heat. When you burn a calorie, a certain amount of heat is generated. If your body is burning lots of calories it is generating lots of heat, which keeps the body temperature up. When the thyroid is burning enough calories and generating enough heat, we are usually able to keep the whole body warm including our hands and feet.

We don't want our fireplace only burning twigs and small branches, we need the fireplace to burn all of the big logs as well, because they give off more heat. This is just like our body, as we don't want to only burn calories from carbohydrates and protein. We need to trigger our body to burn calories from fats, because just like those logs, they give off two and a half times more energy. Don't assume because you're exercising and burning calories that you're burning calories from fat. As we already discussed in the previous chapter, our hormones (adrenals) are very involved in determining which logs go into the fireplace.

Basal Metabolic Rate

A great test to determine how well and efficient your body is burning calories is to measure your metabolism (the rate at which your body burns calories) and get a fix on your basic metabolic rate. Your Basal Metabolic Rate (BMR) is a function of your thyroid and determines the fewest number of calories your body burns to keep you living and breathing. How many calories does your body burn just to live and breathe? We don't want to measure how many calories you burn when you exercise. We want to know how many calories your metabolism is burning at rest. What is your basal metabolic rate? Remember, you only exercise one or two hours a day. The other twenty-two or twenty-three hours your body is basically at rest in a resting, digesting mode.

The amount of calories (heat generated) your body burns if you lay in bed all day is considered your Basal Metabolic Rate. Think of your BMR like the idle speed of your car. If you let the car idle at 1,200 rpms it will burn gasoline at a certain rate. If you increase that idle speed, by stepping on the accelerator, up to 1,500 rpms, it will burn gasoline at a much faster rate. This is what you want to happen in your body. We need to have our thyroid (metabolism) burning more calories for a successful weight loss program. This will help you reach your goals of losing the weight and keeping it off.

Testing the Thyroid

There are two simple tests you can do at home which may gives us a clue how our thyroid is functioning. The first test is very simple. You take an iodine tincture, which can be purchased at any local drugstore.

Place a small stain the size of a quarter on the underside of your forearm. If the stain remains for 18-24 hours, it's a good sign your thyroid may not be the problem. However, if the stain disappears and is absorbed within a few hours that is a clue your thyroid may not be functioning well. Your body needed any available iodine and absorbed all it found from that iodine stain. Placing iodine on your skin is not the best way to nourish your thyroid, rather use a supplement.

The second functional test uses a thermometer to measure your body temperature. Dr. Broda Barnes, an endocrinologist, did years of research on thyroid function and found that measuring your underarm (axillary) temperature was a more accurate way of determining body temperature and an excellent way to determine functional status of the thyroid. This simple test will let you know if you are generating enough heat to keep your core temperature stable. If you are burning an adequate supply of calories your body temperature should be between 97.8 and 98.2 degrees. If your body temperature is below this range this could be a clue that your thyroid may be under-active.

The most important part of this test is that it needs to be done first thing in the morning before you get out of bed. We are trying to determine your basic metabolic rate (body temperature) before you get up, walk around, eat and allow the anxiety of your daily life to kick in. Daily activity will increase your metabolic rate and cause your body temperature to rise. What surprises many patients when doing this underarm test in the middle of the day after indulging in all kinds of activity is that their body temperature is still on the low side. What do you think that tells them? If your body temperature is low in the middle of the day, there is a good chance it is low first thing in the morning and we could be dealing with a thyroid problem.

The second part of this test, besides being done before you get out of bed, is that it needs to be done for at least five days in a row to get a good accurate measurement. Take the average and determine if your body temperature is between 97.8 and 98.2 degrees. The five-day test applies to men and post-menopausal women. If you are still menstruating, I would recommend doing the test for 30 days and then average it out. Some hormones fluctuate during your cycle, which is why you measure yourself for 30 days. Both of these tests are simple and easy to do at home and are meant to give you an indication as to the functional status of your thyroid.

Revving the Engine

There are four things we can do to increase our metabolism. The first is get some exercise! When we exercise and build muscle we increase our metabolism. The reason for this is simple; muscle tissue is metabolically more active than adipose (fat) tissue. This means that a pound of muscle burns more calories than a pound of fat. It's as if we are keeping our foot on the accelerator and revving the engine throughout the day when we exercise. So, if you add additional muscle to your body you will be increasing your metabolism. This is why we want to stimulate our muscles and begin some type of daily exercise routine.

Secondly, eat! When we limit our daily intake of food to one or two meals a day we start slowing down our metabolism. The body has a survival mode. It recognizes that it is only getting food, (calories) twice a day and begins to preserve those calories and burns them more slowly. Therefore, eating only one or two meals a day in hopes of losing weight will cause our metabolism and thyroid to slow down. Whereas, if you feed your body 3-5 times a day it stimulates your metabolism to continually burn calories. Therefore, if you're not eating at least three meals a day, it's like swimming upstream. It will be more difficult to lose weight. Consuming 3-5 meals a day will increase our metabolism and burn a greater number of calories but I know eating more than three meals a day is difficult for some people.

FYI - excess calcium can cause the thyroid and our metabolism to slow down. It is important to look for a calcium supplement that has magnesium, vitamin D and boron. Calcium should be consumed at a ratio of no more than two to one with respect to magnesium. If you take 1,000 mg. of calcium I suggest you get at least 500 mg. of magnesium. These two minerals are effectively absorbed when taken at a 2:1 ratio. Excess calcium that is not absorbed can begin to calcify and plaque the arteries, which is known as hardening of the arteries. If it doesn't do that, it could begin to calcify in our joints, which can contribute to arthritis. Lastly, it can slow down our metabolism.

Those of you who are swallowing antacids for heartburn, indigestion, bloating and gas and are combining calcium to help with osteoporosis may not be getting the benefits you think because an acidic environment is necessary to activate and make calcium, magnesium and other minerals absorbable. Unfortunately, antacids suppress the acidity in the stomach, which interferes with the absorption of these minerals.

Third, various herbal supplements act as thermogenics, which work to heat up the body. The herbs that are shown to work the best at raising our metabolism are ma haung (ephedra) and caffeine. Both are classified as stimulants to the body. Therefore, some precaution must be taken when used. These two herbs are commonly found in many of the weight loss supplements that are on the market today. The drawback for many of us who use these supplements for weight loss is that these two herbs, ma haung and caffeine, are known to deplete and further exhaust the adrenal glands. If you are concerned that you have already exhausted your adrenal glands and are working to nourish them, realize these two herbs will be working against you and should be avoided.

As we discussed earlier, when the adrenal glands are in a state of exhaustion, this inhibits the burning of calories from stored body fat. We may burn more calories with these stimulants, but are those calories coming from the break down of fats? They may promote the break down of proteins (muscle) and carbohydrates due to adrenal exhaustion.

A fourth solution to help with increasing our metabolism and BMR is to look for an underlying problem with the adrenal glands, caused by stress. Excess cortisol, due to stress, will interfere with the production of our thyroid hormones. Think of it like dominos. If the "adrenal domino" falls first, it may knock over and pull down the functional ability of the "thyroid domino." In which case, you need to lift up (support) the "adrenal domino" before you can raise, (repair) the "thyroid domino." Many times the exhaustion of the adrenal glands cause a domino effect to our good health. Various health complaints are sometimes the result of another imbalance from within the body. Therefore, the over production of the stress hormones, (cortisol in particular) caused by constant, excessive stress, could be interfering with the proper function and regulation of the thyroid. This can explain why so many people have an under active thyroid and are taking medications, but not getting the expected results from their medications. Look for a possible under-lying adrenal problem. If you don't fix that first, all the medications or supplements that work to raise your metabolism and BMR may be unsuccessful. Look to the adrenal glands first! This is not to say that it couldn't be an actual thyroid problem, in which case we need to strengthen and support the thyroid.

Finally nourish and strengthen the thyroid with nutrition and supplementation. Iodine found from kelp is an excellent source of nourishment for the thyroid. Tyrosine, B-vitamins, selenium, zinc and thyroid glandulars should also be included in a nutrition protocol to support the thyroid.

Summary

- The thyroid regulates our metabolism and the rate we burn calories.
- A calorie is a unit of heat.
- Increasing our metabolism promotes the breakdown of additional calories and helps with weight lose.
- Our metabolism can be increased by
  - Exercising
  - Eating a minimum of 3-5 meals a day
  - Using herbal thermogenics
  - Nourishing the adrenal glands and thyroid
- Energy is generated from the break down of fats, carbo-hydrates and protein.

Action Steps

- Do iodine and axillary temperature test.
- Begin an exercise program and find ways to stimulate your muscles daily.
- Eat 3-5 meals a day.
- Nourish the thyroid and adrenals if you suspect they need assistance.

Chapter Five

Balancing Blood Sugar

The first part of the book has covered the importance of stress and how stress can trigger certain hormones. We've reviewed how certain hormones can trigger the break down of fats, proteins and carbohydrates in response to stress. We discussed that oftentimes people complain that they are not getting the desired results from their time, energy and efforts they spend dieting and exercising. I have always said that if it's not your diet or exercise program, then it must be your hormones caused by stress. I want to begin discussing how diet triggers our hormones and how they can work in our favor or against us.

Suppose you had a thousand dollars a month to invest and you could invest in anything you wanted - stocks, bonds, real estate, jewelry or whatever. One of the most important considerations is the rate of return on your investment. Would you rather invest your hard earned money into some investment that will give you a return on your investment of 5-10% or would you rather invest your money into something that would return 40-50% on your investment, the amount of risk being equal?

It's pretty obvious - this is a no brainer. However, to use the old cliché, "time is money!" We need to recognize and acknowledge that our time is valuable and whatever time we have to spend on dieting and working out, we should try to optimize our investment. Are we getting the most out of the time, energy and effort we spend each week counting calories, fat grams, watching our diet and working out?

If you are not getting the results you want, you need to make some changes. The problem could be your diet, your workouts or both, assuming that your stress hormones are in balance. However, there is another old saying that says the definition of insanity is doing the same thing over and over again, hoping for a different result. If what you are doing isn't working then try something else.

First, it is important to understand the benefits we receive from our time and efforts come from three separate areas. Approximately 20% of the benefits we receive from exercise come from the actual physical workout; 20% of the benefits from exercise are derived from rest and recuperation. While at least 60% of our benefits from exercise come from our diet. That's right - diet!

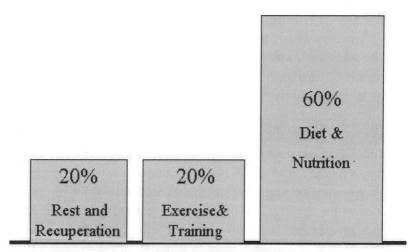

Where do you invest your time, energy and effort?

With that in mind we need to ask ourselves, in what area are we investing most of our time, energy and efforts? Are we investing wisely in the area that has the greatest rate of return, our diet? Are we investing wisely with our money and poorly with our health?

Are the results we get from our workouts as visible as we would like them to be? Perhaps we need to reevaluate and adjust our diet to seek the greatest return for our weight loss efforts.

The Importance of Diet

With at least 60% of the results from our exercise routine coming from our diet, we need to discuss the importance of diet and how to make our diets work for us. First and foremost, when I use the word diet - I do not use the word "diet" in reference to a restrictive weight loss plan of eating. When I use the word "diet," I am simply stating the food and drink we place in our body to maintain existence. When we go to the zoo and ask what is the typical diet for the lions, tigers and bears, we are not thinking they are on some restrictive weight loss program. We are simply trying to determine what lions, tigers and bears eat to maintain their existence, and not what type of restrictive dieting program are they on.

Let me first emphasize, diets in the traditional sense don't work! I want to share with you how the body functions, how our blood sugar controls our hormones and how these hormones impact whether or not we burn or store fat. We need to be wise in this area of our investment, especially since the return is so high.

First and foremost, when it comes to determining a healthy eating or dieting program, it is of utmost importance to follow a dieting or eating program that is healthy and can be maintained for the rest of your life. If the dieting program you're following isn't healthy and something you cannot do long-term, you won't succeed. For example, if you follow a restrictive eating program to lose weight, there is a good chance that once you reach your desired goal and you didn't learn any lifestyle changes to promote better health, you will probably regain the weight again. If the dieting plan you're on doesn't promote good health, stay away from it. These are your typical fad diets where you eat or drink certain foods all day long like shakes, pineapples, watermelon or grapefruits. Although they may help you lose weight, it may not be weight loss from the breakdown of fat. Furthermore, it may not be nutritionally healthy, meaning it does not supply your body with all the **vitamins, mineral, antioxidants, fatty acids, fiber and good bacteria** that are the building blocks for good health.

Does your weight loss and dieting program emphasize eating 4-6 meals a day, which is more than you have time for in your day? If that is the case, there is a good chance that once you reach your weight loss goal, you may no longer follow a dieting program of 4-6 meals a day and revert back to 2-3 meals a day and regain your weight. Eating 4-6 meals a day increases the metabolism, but you may be like many of us and don't have time to eat 4-6 meals in a day. Perhaps it would be easier to learn how to make our body continue to burn calories from fat on three meals a day, because patient compliance is a major part of success for any weight loss program.

Counting Carbohydrates and Fats

Let's first bury the myth about fat in our diet. Most people in the last 25 years have been led to believe that fat is bad for our body. We have been told that we eat too much fatty food and that this is the leading cause of obesity, heart disease, stroke and cancer in our society. For the past 25 years we have been eating more calories from carbohydrates and less from fats. While at the same time our rate of obesity, heart disease, stroke, cancer and diabetes is increasing. Let me clearly state that fat is not the culprit it has been made out to be; it is not bad for us, and is in fact, essential for our existence. There are some fats that are worse than others, which is why we need to look at different types of fats. There are many cultures that eat more fats than North Americans, yet don't have the same health problems. This is why balancing our fat intake with respect to carbohydrates and proteins are important.

There are three major nutrients we consume each day - carbohydrates, proteins and fats. Most people know when we eat carbohydrates we break the carbohydrates down into sugar and produce energy. Proteins are broken down and used to produce muscle. However, many people believe that the fat we eat has no purpose, except for taste and to make us heavier.

In the last chapter, we showed how the body uses fats as a raw material to make hormones. If you have been following a low fat or no fat diet regimen and not getting the results you have been expecting, and also suffer with **PMS, menopause, arthritis, heart disease or headaches**, it may have something to do with the proper amount of fats, specifically the ratio of saturated and monounsaturated fats in your diet. Are we eating enough of the good fats, (monounsaturated, omega-3 & omega-6 fatty acids) in our diet? Do we overload our body with saturated fats, which when out of balance can create health problems?

The real problem isn't just the fats in our diet, but rather the excessive sugar (carbohydrates) consumption and what it does to our blood sugar levels! This blood sugar balance is another piece of the puzzle that needs to be intact to achieve long lasting and successful weight loss.

Don't think that I am down on carbohydrates! I am a big believer in the importance and necessity of carbohydrates. I am a big fan of the carbohydrates we get from fruits, vegetables and whole grains. What I am concerned about is the over-consumption of refined carbohydrates (processed white flour and processed white sugar), which have become a major staple in today's society, and the consequences they have on our bodies' ability to regulate our blood sugar. Since "The Garden of Eden" until modern times, all the foods we have eaten have been organic and unrefined. Organic food was not something that was started by a bunch of hippies back in the 60's out in California. It's been in the last century with the invention of food processing that our diet has been drastically disturbed and has changed the ratio of carbohydrates to proteins to fats in our diet.

These refined carbohydrates have been triggering our blood sugar level to skyrocket up and down, which causes hormonal imbalance.

Patient Story

Beverly was a self-admitted carbohydrate junkie who had struggled with her weight for years. For years she had been eating low-fat and no-fat, fearing that fats would make her gain even more weight. Her typical breakfast was a cup of coffee with a bagel or muffin, on others days a bowl of cereal. Lunch was yogurt, rice cakes, crackers, microwave popcorn, or pretzels. She would have a soft drink or cup of coffee to make it through the rest of her day and dinner was usually lots of pasta and breads.

She complained not only of an inability to lose weight but also of low blood sugar, irritability if meals were skipped or delayed, fatigue, light headedness, PMS, difficulty with her periods, sensitivity to bright lights and food cravings.

After reviewing her symptoms and diet history, we eliminated refined carbohydrates (foods that are prepackaged with processed white flour and white sugar) from her diet and replaced them with meals that had more protein and good fat. We were trying to stabilize her hormones and not overload the release of insulin. Within a couple of days, her energy level picked up, her cravings subsided and her need to eat every 2-3 hours was reduced. She wasn't having that drained feeling at mid-afternoon, her periods were less severe, and her weight finally began to drop.

Beverly had been eating so many carbohydrates each day that it was throwing her hormones out of balance and triggering the wrong responses. The body needs carbohydrates; we just need to make sure we don't overload ourselves with too many carbohydrates or the wrong (refined) carbohydrates.

Balancing our blood sugar is vital in a successful weight lose program. The goal is to restore the body back to balance. Surely, we understand the importance of a balanced diet of carbohydrates, proteins and fats. If the body is out of balance, an unbalanced diet may be required to restore balance. Think of it as a scale, if one side is out of balance and you add equal weight to both sides, the scale will still be out of balance. However, if you add more weight to one side than the other it will begin to rebalance the scale. If our blood sugar levels are out of balance and triggering weight gain and other health problems a balanced diet may not be the appropriate diet to follow at this time. An imbalanced dieting protocol may be needed in order to restore balance back to the body. Once balance is restored and our health is back than we should consume a more balanced diet.

Balancing our Blood Sugar

The two hormones we need to pay close attention to in our quest for losing weight and balancing our blood sugar are insulin and glucagon. These two hormones are controlled by diet. What we eat will trigger the release of insulin and glucagon. The role they play is immense and the balance they maintain can make or break our dieting efforts. Most of us are familiar with insulin because of the association it has with diabetes. However, many of us are unfamiliar with glucagon and the role it plays in balancing our blood sugar and promoting the breakdown of fats. When the production of one hormone is up the other is down and vice-a-versa. They both work at balancing our blood sugar. Insulin will lower blood sugar, while glucagon will raise our blood sugar.

Let's start simple. Insulin is considered an "anabolic" hormone. The definition of anabolic is to grow or to build. The hormone glucagon is considered a "catabolic" hormone, which means to breakdown or tear apart. If you are trying to lose weight and keep the weight off, you should be striving to trigger your body to produce a good balance of both the anabolic and catabolic hormones.

Insulin   Glucagon

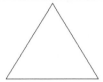

A proper diet promotes the availability of both insulin and glucagon.

The question you need to be asking is what triggers these responses? Do certain foods trigger the release of one hormone over the other? Do we release enough glucagon to promote the breakdown of fats? Will some foods trigger our body to burn fat and other foods to store fat? Can we control certain hormonal responses, which promotes weight loss?

Your daily food selection can have a huge affect on your hormones. Depending on what you eat affects hormonal balance. Diet controls these responses! Let's first discuss how certain meals can promote balance of these two hormones and how certain food selections can promote an imbalance. Then we will explain what happens when we eat a meal.

If you look at the typical American diet over the last 20 years, it has more or less been a diet of low fat or no fat. In that same time period, we have increased the number of people complaining of heart disease, stroke, diabetes, obesity, high cholesterol, high blood pressure, arthritis, menopause PMS etc. We have been led to believe that the problem is fat or excessive fat in our diet. However, if you look at other cultures around the world that eat more fat in their daily diet than Americans do, they do not have the same health complaints - it just doesn't add up!

On paper it looks as though fats could be the problem. A gram of fat is converted into nine calories. A gram of protein or carbohydrate only produces four calories apiece. When you start adding up and counting how many calories we are ingesting at each meal, we see that calories from fats can really start to add up. This is why for years people have been trying to count calories to lose weight. Who wants to spend all of their time in front of a scale or looking at conversion charts to see how many calories they have eaten? I've heard that counting calories only helps your arithmetic skills!

If we only look at the fat grams or calorie content in our daily meal selections, we are making a mistake. Looking at only fats and calories to determine if we can eat them is like looking at someone's IQ or financial status to determine if you want to be friends with them. We don't pick our friends based solely on these two criteria, nor should we be picking our food based solely on their fat or caloric content.

If it was just fats and calories that were the cause of our obesity problems and many other health complaints that are associated with obesity, then how can we explain the "French Paradox"? It is called the "French Paradox" because the French eat much more fatty foods than Americans, yet they don't experience the same rate of obesity, heart disease, stroke, diabetes and other ailments that Americans do. They are eating lots of cheese, sour cream, butter, eggs and dairy in their diet. Great tasting stuff, but they are all considered no no's in the American diet. This could help explain why obesity and other health related problems do not come strictly from too much fat, but instead come from too much sugar (refined carbohydrates) in our daily diet.

The fats that are bad for us are the partially hydrogenated fats or "trans" fatty acids as they are called. These are the fats that are not beneficial for promoting good health. You can usually find the partially hydrogenated fats in many baked or prepackaged foods. Many of the condiments that we use are loaded with these "trans" fatty acids. Read your labels. If the ingredient list contains partially hydrogenated fats, try to avoid them.

Carbohydrates Do What!

Let's talk about what happens when we eat a meal and the triggering mechanisms that come into play. First, we will talk about the effects carbohydrates have on insulin production. As we have been told for the last 25 years - eat no fat or low fat foods and eat more carbohydrates. If we don't provide enough good fats, (essential fatty acids) due to restricted fat intake we can be creating an imbalance of all our hormones, which are involved in all areas of our life not just our reproductive system. Therefore, if you complain of PMS, menopause, arthritis or headaches and have been on a low or no fat diet, I would recommend supplementing your diet with some essential fatty acids (omega-3 and omega-6).

When we eat carbohydrates, the sugar from the carbohydrate is released into our bloodstream. Our blood sugar levels increase in response to carbohydrates in our meal. This triggers the pancreas to produce insulin in order to lower our blood sugar levels. Insulin works by pushing the sugar out of our blood stream and into the cells, where they can be utilized for energy. This is a beneficial task.

If we keep these hormones in balance we do a better job of controlling our blood sugar. The problem is if the food is heavily loaded with carbohydrates, especially refined, processed carbohydrates, then the blood sugar will elevate quite rapidly and surge very high. If the blood sugar increases rapidly, the pancreas will respond with a huge production of insulin to lower the blood sugar. If our blood sugar skyrockets up, it will then roller coaster down very fast because of the effects of insulin. It is that roller coaster ride down where many of our problems begin such as, low blood sugar, food cravings, fatigue, irritability, moodiness, lightheadedness and/or irritability if meals are skipped or delayed. The body prefers to keep the blood sugar fairly level. Those blood sugar surges caused by a diet high in carbohydrates are difficult to stabilize. This excessive sugar in the diet will also heavily tax our adrenal glands, which is an additional stress that must be dealt with.

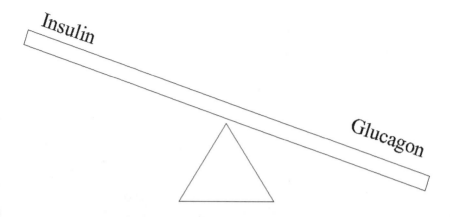

A diet high in carbohydrates causes insulin to increase.

Since insulin is considered an anabolic hormone, its effects are to make us bigger. Not necessarily bigger and stronger but probably bigger and fatter if we don't properly control our insulin response. Insulin also works as a storage hormone. Insulin will take the excess carbohydrates and store them as fat.

The breakdown of a meal is relatively simple. Carbohydrates are sugars that are converted into glucose and used for energy. The problem is that we can only utilize so many carbohydrates at each meal. The rest will be stored. Some of it will be stored as glycogen, which is a stored form of sugar found in the liver and skeletal muscles. The rest of the carbohydrates are stored as fat

Insulin stores excess carbohydrates as fat. The body doesn't store all those carbohydrates as sugar. Some carbohydrates will be stored as sugar, some will be stored as fat. If you're eating meals loaded with carbohydrates and you're having problems with weight loss, maybe the foods you're eating are triggering a hormonal response that is storing fats.

Another problem with high carbohydrate meals that produce a high insulin response is that those excess carbohydrates that are stored, as fats will increase your triglyceride count. If your blood work shows a high triglyceride count, reduce the intake of refined and processed carbohydrates. This will usually take care of the problem.

Patient Story

Walter came to me complaining of type II Adult onset diabetes, inability to lose weight and a high triglyceride count. He was only 33 years of age, somewhat active but was taking oral medication to control his diabetes and was advised at his last physical that his "HDL" (good cholesterol) was low and his triglycerides were high.

Walters diet consisted mostly of carbohydrates. Most of his carbohydrates came from refined and processed foods. We immediately reduced his carbohydrates and increased the protein and good fats in his diet. Within a few days, he noticed that his blood sugar had begun to stabilize and his medication needed to be adjusted. Since he wasn't eating so many carbohydrates he didn't need so much medication to control his insulin. He was feeling better within the first few weeks and a couple of months later he had lost almost twenty pounds. His lab work showed that his triglycerides and good cholesterol were now in normal ranges.

The overload of carbohydrates to his body provoked a domino effect to his health. All of those excess carbohydrates were stored as fat, which created more stress to his heart health.

Think about this the next time you try to load up with a high carbohydrate meal. What do you think ranchers feed their cattle to get them as fat as possible before they are sold at market? They are fed strictly carbohydrates (grains), which increase their blood sugar and insulin. This overload of insulin triggers the body to convert the excess sugar into fat. Keeping them in pens prevents them from walking (exercising) around and burning off any stored carbohydrates and fats. A great tasting steak is marbled with fat. Ranchers are not feeding their cattle ice cream and cookies to fatten them up. They are letting them eat more and more grains, which eventually cause hormonal imbalance and makes the cow fatter.

This is the same thing that happens to us when we continually eat a diet high in carbohydrates, especially refined carbohydrates. Maybe that visual will help us turn away from some of the high carbohydrate rich meals that most Americans follow. These include meal selections such as bagels, muffins, cereals, breads, pancakes, crackers, popcorn, rice cakes, pasta, pretzels, tortilla chips, baked potatoes, fruit juices and coffee. These are all foods that are very common in our diet and are considered good choices by some of the same experts who think fats are the problem. However, all of the above named foods are known to rapidly increase the release of insulin, which start the rollercoaster ride for our blood sugar.

The Effects of Glucagon

The second hormone we need to pay attention to when it comes to losing weight and balancing our blood sugar is glucagon. We can't control our body by simply talking to it and telling it to burn fats, proteins or carbohydrates. We can't tell our body to burn only stored fat and leave the muscle alone. That would be just like the Tiger Woods commercial where he tells the ball to fly 350 yards, with a slight fade and land softly on the green. It just doesn't happen that way or at least not for me. If it did, we wouldn't have the problem of obesity that we currently have. Instead we'd all be looking down at our bellies and backsides saying "burn baby, burn."

There is always a triggering mechanism involved. Insulin is triggered in direct response to the amount of carbohydrates consumed. Therefore, insulin triggers the body to burn calories from the sugars and carbohydrates found in the foods we just ate. Insulin does not trigger the body to burn calories from stored body fat, it triggers the body to store fat and it inhibits the release of an enzyme that is crucial for fat metabolism. However, glucagon does trigger the body to burn calories from those stored sources of carbohydrates and fats.

Glucagon is a catabolic hormone. Its production is inhibited by the production of insulin. If you have a large amount of insulin circulating in the blood stream, due to a high carbohydrate meal, your body will not be able to produce glucagon. Insulin inhibits the production of glucagon.

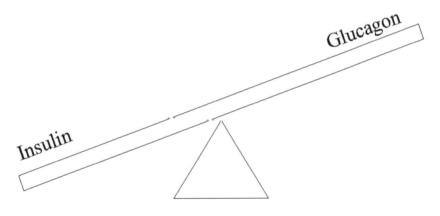

**A low carbohydrate meal with more protein and fat
causes glucagon to increase.**

After a meal high in carbohydrates, a huge insulin spike is produced to lower our blood sugar. Three to four hours pass by and all that insulin has completely lowered your blood sugar to an abnormally low level. We know that when our blood sugar is low we suffer from food cravings, irritability, mood swings, inability to concentrate, muscle weakness and the list goes on. Does your body produce enough glucagon after your meals to burn calories from fats and keep your blood sugar stable?

If the meal has a moderate amount of carbohydrates, a more balanced response of both insulin and glucagon occurs. This helps keep the blood sugar from going too high or too low. Therefore, the proper balance of glucagon and insulin is controlled by our food choices. This is why it's important that our meals are not overloaded with carbohydrates, because it will not trigger the release of glucagon, which is vital for maintaining our blood sugar.

The reason our blood sugar causes all those symptoms like food cravings, irritability, light-headedness, moodiness, nervousness and inability to think or concentrate is because the brains only source of energy comes from the breakdown of sugar (glucose). Thus, when the blood sugar is abnormally low, the brain's fuel source is also low, which causes us to function poorly. That's why it's vital to maintain a level blood sugar count.

Glycemix Index

Now that you know carbohydrates trigger your body to release insulin, which stores fat, we need to learn which foods trigger the greatest insulin response and keep those foods to a minimum. A glycemix index will help us with this concern.

The glycemix index is a measurement of how quickly sugar is broken down and released into the blood stream. Foods that release a high amount of sugar into the blood stream are the ones that trigger the huge insulin response, which are the ones we want to stay away from. Foods that are considered low or moderately low on the glycemix index allow for the release of glucagon, which helps stabilize our blood sugar and promotes healthy weight loss.

Table sugar or sucrose is released very rapidly into our bloodstream and causes a huge rise in our blood sugar level. Foods made from refined white flour and refined white sugar cause a larger spike in our blood sugar level than unrefined flour and sugar. The carbohydrates (sugar) from an apple are released more slowly and cause a much smaller surge in our blood sugar compared to popcorn or rice cakes. Foods that are high in protein and fat (pecans, seeds, eggs, meat, chicken, fish) do not contain many carbohydrates and will not cause much of a spike in our blood sugar level.

The name of the game is to select foods from the chart below that are known to cause a low to moderate surge in our blood sugar level. You may be surprised to find out many of the foods you have been eating are foods that may be working against your natural hormonal response. What you will typically find is that foods that come in a box or package usually trigger a larger release of insulin than raw fruits and vegetables.

Glycemic Index

Foods are rated according to how fast the carbohydrates are broken down and cause our blood sugar level to rise. To better control our blood sugar levels, it is recommended to eat foods from the Low and Medium category and consume only on occasion the foods from the high and very high category.

Glycemix Ratings: L = Low, M = Medium, H = High, VH = Very High

Low
Apples, Asparagus, Broccoli, Celery, Cherries, Cucumbers, Fructose, Grapefruit, Green Pepper, Lettuce, Onion, Peach, Pear, Plum, Spinach, Strawberries, Tomato, Zucchini

Medium
Baked Beans, Cantaloupe, Grapes, Lactose, Oatmeal, Oranges, Pasta, Peaches, Pear, Pineapples, Pinto beans, Sweet Potato, Watermelons, Yam

High

Bagel, Banana, Bread, Cereals (whole grains), Carrots, Corn/Corn chips, Muffins, Granola, Porridge, White Potato, Pretzels, Raisins, Rice, Sucrose, Tortilla/Tortilla chips

Very High

Cereals (Processed/Refined), Glucose, Honey, Maltose, Plain Crackers, Popcorn, Rice Cakes, White bread

With a basic knowledge and better understanding of how the body functions, we can now look at how the American diet has failed and why the rate of heart disease, stroke, diabetes and obesity is on the rise. Most Americans are told to eat more carbohydrates and less fat in their diet. People are choosing to eat low fat or no fat and are replacing those calories with additional carbohydrates. This high ratio of carbohydrates to fats and proteins leads to hormonal imbalance. These additional carbohydrates are being stored as fat! The body can only use so many carbohydrates at one time. Additional carbohydrates are converted to fat. The large amount of sugar in our bloodstream will trigger the body to release huge amounts of insulin. The constant huge amounts of insulin (hyperinsulinema), being released into our bloodstream will inhibit the release of glucagon. No Glucagon! No Fat Burning! No fat burning means no long - term success on a weight loss program.

Stress, Blood Sugar & Weight Loss

Balancing your blood sugar is vital to promote healthy weight loss. It is extremely important if you are also suffering from stage two or three of functional adrenal exhaustion. If you feel that you have over-taxed your adrenal glands it is important to eliminate or reduce the use of refined sugars from your diet. This will only exaggerate the stress on the adrenal glands. Since the adrenal glands are involved with controlling blood sugar, it only makes it more difficult if you keep causing your adrenal glands to constantly work due to any large fluctuations in your blood sugar.

The other effect cortisol has on insulin is that it combats the effectiveness of insulin, which leads to an even greater production of insulin that can eventually lead to insulin resistance and or diabetes. Insulin resistance is when the cells of your body are unable to recognize the insulin molecules. This is typically a result of a diet high in refined carbohydrates. The huge amount of insulin in our blood sugar causes the cells to become more resistant to insulin, which in turn leads to further production of insulin. It is that constant surge of insulin that is damaging to our health and it is a diet loaded with refined carbohydrates that continues that cycle.

Many people who suffer from Type II, adult onset diabetes are taking medications not because their pancreas isn't making enough insulin but rather their pancreas cannot keep on making the huge amounts of insulin caused by a diet high in refined carbohydrates. This is why diet and exercise can control diabetes. If you're not causing your blood sugar to surge very high, your body won't have to produce so much insulin. Secondly, when you exercise (walking is a great exercise) you make the cells of your body more sensitive to insulin, which helps keep your blood sugar from going to high.

Summary

- 60% of the benefits from exercise come from our diet.
- Fats are not the main problem that causes weight gain.
- Control our blood sugar level helps our weight loss efforts.
- The types of foods we eat will determine our blood sugar level.
- Insulin lowers our blood sugar and promotes the storage of fats.
- Glucagon raises blood sugar and promotes the break down of fats.
- Insulin is produced in response to carbohydrates in the meal.
- Insulin inhibits the release of glucagon.
- Choose foods from the glycemix Index that are considered low to moderate with regards to their release of insulin.

Action Steps

- Evaluate the hormonal response your diet causes to your body.
- Choose foods that promote blood sugar stability.
- Reduce or eliminate refined carbohydrates from your diet.

Chapter Six

The Five & Two Plan

The dieting plans I recommend are very simple to follow. For five days out of the week treat your body like a temple and for two days treat it like an amusement park. What I mean is, for five days eat a healthy, balanced, nutritious diet. If you need to take a break and reward yourself for five days of good eating, you can go ahead and eat less healthy on two days. I call it the Five & Two plan. Most people find it easier to eat healthy during the week and reward themselves with desserts and other junk foods that are not meant to promote good health during the weekend. I am not a total killjoy.

The goal is to have more good days of dieting than bad days. If we diet well for five days and do poorly for two days at least we had more good days of dieting than bad. We took more steps in the right direction with our diet by choosing to have more good days of dieting than bad. Of course it would be better to take seven steps in the right direction with our dieting plan, but mental anguish and feelings of deprivation and boredom take over our thinking.

When people do a good job of dieting for five days they often times look forward to rewarding themselves with something sinfully delicious on those two other days. The goal is to treat your body like a temple and diet well for those five days. Then you feel justified for earning your reward for an amusement park day. You can't or you shouldn't go to the amusement (sweets, cookies, candies, desserts, junk food, etc...) park every day, you need to earn that right. Therefore, treat your body right for five days and earn the trips to the amusement park.

Also, for hundreds of centuries people have lived a healthy life without the need of counting calories or weighing out their proportions. I don't believe in making people do more for themselves than I would do for myself. If you follow the Five & Two plan with these Ten Steps for better dieting, you will begin to lose weight and get healthier.

Ten Steps for Healthy Eating

1. Regulate your blood sugar with the proper balance of insulin and glucagon.
2. Reduce or eliminate refined white flour and sugars from with your meal.
3. Eat a fiber rich diet.
4. Avoid partially hydrogenated fats, artificial sweeteners, preservatives and colors.
5. Raw nuts, seeds and fruits are excellent snack foods.
6. Drink only a few ounces of water with your meal.
7. Eat organic as much as possible.
8. Combine your food appropriately.
9. Don't ruin a healthy nutritious meal with an unhealthy dessert.
10. Relax and enjoy your meal.

Step One - Regulate your blood sugar with the proper balance of insulin and glucagon.
- Eat good protein and fats with each meal.
- Protein and fat slows down the release of insulin and allows glucagon to be released into our bloodstream.
- Protein rich foods are found in eggs, chicken, seafood, beef, pork, lamb and wild game.
- The availability of glucagon promotes the break down of fats.
- Good fats to eat are the monounsaturated fats (omega-3 and omega-6).

- Good fats are found in coldwater fish (salmon, mackerel, halibut, cod, sardines), nuts and seeds and various oils (olive, flax, canola, sesame, safflower, evening primrose and cod liver oil).

Step Two - Reduce or eliminate refined white flour and white sugar.
- Foods that are made with processed flours and sugars trigger larger release of insulin and throw your blood sugar further out of balance.
- Most prepackaged food is highly refined. Stay away from foods that come in a box or wrapped in plastic.
- 100% whole grain, unrefined foods should replace your current foods that are made with highly refined white flour and sugar.

Step Three - Eat a diet rich in fiber.
- Constipation is the unspoken common problem of today that causes internal pollution of your body.
- Eat a raw salad a day.
- Eat 5-7 servings of fruits, vegetables and whole grains.

Step Four - Nuts, seeds and fruits make excellent snacks.
- Almonds, pecans, walnuts, macadamia, cashews, sunflower seeds, flax seeds etc. are a great source of omega 3 & 6 fatty acids.
- Nuts and seeds can easily be added to cereal, oatmeal and yogurt to help slow down the release of insulin from a meal loaded with carbohydrates.
- Fruits are better to eat by themselves.
- Many people are sensitive to peanuts, stay away from peanuts if you suspect candida or fungal yeast overgrowth.

Step Five - Avoid partially hydrogenated fats, artificial sweeteners and preservatives.
- Partially hydrogenated fats are found in many baked and prepackaged food.
- They have been chemically altered from their natural state and are more difficult for the body to process.
- Margarine is a partially hydrogenated fat. Butter is better.

- Artificial sweeteners have not shown any proof that they contribute to weight loss, and many people show sensitivity to these artificial sweeteners.
- Artificial preservatives, colors, dyes and flavoring are all chemicals that we are ingesting and contribute to chemical stress.

Step Six - Drink only a few ounces (2-6 ounces) of water with your meal.

- The body produces enzymes to digest and break down food.
- When we ingest large amounts of fluids with our meals (water, tea, soda, coffee or juices), we dilute the concentration and effectiveness of these enzymes.
- Bloating, gas, heartburn, indigestion or reflux could be caused by excessive fluid in your meal.
- Drink 8-10 glasses of water a day, just don't drink them with your meal.

Step Seven - Eat as much organic and unrefined food as possible.

- Since the "Garden of Eden" we have eaten organic food.
- Foods loaded with antibiotics, insecticides, pesticides and other harsh chemicals are taxing to the body.

Step Eight - Combine your foods properly.

- Certain foods combine better than other foods.
- Proteins do not combine well with starchy carbohydrates (potato, corn, rice, beans, breads).This does not mean they cannot be eaten together, only that it is more difficult to digest.
- Proteins combine well with fibrous vegetables (broccoli, spinach, asparagus, squash, zucchini and other green leafy vegetables)
- Eat fruits by themselves.
- Proper food combining can eliminate indigestion, bloating, gas- and heartburn.
- No other animal on earth eats as humans do. We like to have five or six different foods on our plate, yet in nature, animals will stop and eat a whole carcass, a whole bunch of leaves or a stalk of bananas at one time. This makes digestion much easier.

Step Nine - Don't ruin a healthy nutritious meal with a bad dessert.
- You are what your body absorbs!
- Don't assume that if you ate it your body absorbed it.
- A second unspoken common complaint is bloating, gas, indigestion and heartburn.
- The absorption of a nutritious healthy meal can be hampered by the addition of a dessert that is loaded with refined sugars, chemicals, sweeteners, flavors and dyes.
- If you want to have a dessert, wait at least an hour and eat it by itself or splurge on your amusement park day.

Step Ten - Relax and enjoy your meal.
- Eating on the run, in a hurry, standing up hinders absorption and can inhibit the production of digestive enzymes, which can lead to bloating, gas, indigestion and heartburn.
- Take the time to enjoy your meal and properly digest your food.

Balancing Carbohydrates, Proteins & Fats

The key to healthy dieting begins with balancing and regulating your blood sugar. A meal high in carbohydrates will trigger the release of insulin. Stay away from foods that are rated "high" and "very high" on the glycemix index. When less carbohydrates and more proteins and fats are eaten, the hormone glucagon is released, which promotes the break down of fats. Glucagon works to raise our blood sugar, while insulin works to lower our blood sugar.

Breakfast

It is called breakfast because when you think about it you are actually "breaking" a mini "fast." Many people choose to skip, scrimp or choose the wrong foods to start their day. Those who skip breakfast completely are making the biggest mistake. Breakfast or lunch should be your largest meal of the day. If most people have their last meal of the day, no later than eight or nine in the evening and then skip breakfast and not eat until mid-morning, they may go 12-14 hours without putting any type of nourishment in their body. Our blood sugar is typically lowest in the morning since we haven't eaten anything for approximately ten to twelve hours. That's a half-day fast! Therefore, we need to "break" that "mini-fast" in the morning with a meal that will nourish our body with enough calories and energy to make our day productive and keep our blood sugar in balance.

Patient Story

Alex was a young health 32 year old who complained of fatigue, irritability and anxiety. He was very athletic and followed a very clean diet. He didn't eat much junk food and ate lots of good proteins, fats and carbohydrates. Every morning he followed a very intense and demanding workout six days a week. He typically didn't eat after eight PM, he wouldn't eat anything before his workout and he wouldn't complete his workout until eight AM. He would have a cup of coffee on his way to work and would not eat until mid-morning if at all.

Since he waits to eat his first meal of the day at mid-morning his blood sugar is completely depleted due to the fact that he hasn't eaten since eight PM the night before. Plus he further compounds that problem with an intense workout that further depletes his blood sugar.

After reviewing this regimen, I suggested he eat some fruit before his morning workout and wait at least twenty minutes before starting his workout. I also advised him to start having breakfast after his workout, in order to replenish his blood sugar and nourish his body. His lack of energy, irritability and anxiety were associated to his low blood sugar caused by his workout and his dietary choices. His complaints lessened when he started to maintain his blood sugar levels.

If you complain of low blood sugar, food cravings, lack of energy, irritability and moodiness if meals are missed or delayed, it is extremely important to get a good start to your day and not let your blood sugar roller coaster up and down by missing breakfast or eating a meal that is loaded with carbohydrates. The everyday cup of coffee and / or bagel for breakfast sends your blood sugar sky high and starts that roller coaster ride the rest of the day with your blood sugar.

A carbohydrate rich meal triggers the release of hormones that have a very sedative, calmative and relaxing effect on the brain, whereas a meal with less carbohydrates and more protein triggers hormones that have a stimulatory and excitatory effect on the brain. This is important particularly if you have a big presentation or test to take, because you need to be thinking as clear as possible. The last thing you want to do is trigger hormones that are going to make your thinking sedate, calm and slow. Therefore, eat a meal that contains more protein and less carbohydrates in order to promote a more alert, excited response.

Meal Suggestions

Eggs - are a great choice for breakfast and can be made so many ways.
• Poached, soft boiled, hard-boiled, scrambled, fried or omelets.
• Omelets are my preferred choice with plenty of vegetables (onions, garlic, cilantro, jalapenos or any veggie you prefer).
• Quiche is another great choice, made with plenty of vegetables.
• 100% Whole grain cereals or oatmeal is another great breakfast choice.

- I recommend eating these carbohydrates rich foods with a handful of nuts; almonds, pecans, walnuts, macadamia, pine or any other kind of nut.
- The fats found in nuts and seeds slow down the release of sugar into our bloodstream. Therefore, whenever eating a food that is considered high or very high on the glycemix index, add a small handful of nuts to slow down the release of sugar. This keeps the insulin from surging so high and help keep our blood sugar from getting out of balance.

Lunch

To avoid that mid-afternoon drop in energy, stay away from a meal loaded with carbohydrates. A combination of protein (fish, chicken, beef, egg, tuna, lamb or pork) and green leafy vegetables make an excellent meal.

- Grilled chicken salad, taco salad (avoid the shell), shrimp salad, a salad with a couple of eggs
- Beef, fish, chicken, tuna with a large salad.
- Beef, fish, chicken, tuna with two to three servings of vegetables (broccoli, spinach, squash and other green leafy vegetables)
- Homemade chili, made with little or no beans.
- Fajitas (beef or chicken), enchiladas and tacos can be eaten, limit the intake of beans and rice and avoid the fried tortilla chips.
- Don't be afraid of avocadoes! We are not a nation of overweight people because we eat too many avocadoes.
- Beef Stew, try to minimize the starchy carbohydrates (potato, corn and carrots) and add some other vegetables.
- Chinese food is fine, limit the noodles and rice and eat plenty of vegetables.
- With Italian food, include protein and limit the pasta.

Dinner

Dinner should be the smallest of your three meals. Unfortunately, it is typically the largest meal for most people. Dinner is usually an extension of lunch. If you want to add more carbohydrates to your meal, let it be at dinner. Remember carbohydrates promote calm, sedate and relaxation in your body, which is what is needed when we begin to unwind and relax when we finish a long day and prepare for bedtime.

Snacks

Should be anything healthy, (nuts, seeds and fruits are great choices).

Summary

- Follow the Five & Two Plan.
- Treat your body like a temple for five days and treat it like an amusement park for two days.
- Eat more good meals than bad meals in a week.
- The more good meals you have in a week compared to bad meals will show how well you are doing with your diet.
- Take more steps forward in the right direction with your diet.

Action Steps

- Learn the Ten Steps for Healthy Dieting and follow them!

Chapter Seven

Exercise & Fitness

A question often asked is do you need to exercise in order to lose weight and keep it off? No, you don't have to exercise to lose weight, but if you want to complement your dieting efforts it will definitely help speed up the process. A second question asked is will my body firm up and tone up as I start to lose weight? No, you will have to do some type of exercise, if you want to add shape and tone to your body.

The first point we need to make about an exercise program is we are not trying to make anybody an athlete! An exercise program is any-thing as simple as walking, stretching or yoga. The more serious athlete may include jogging, cycling, swimming, aerobic dance or weight training. Our goal is to incorporate physical activity into our lifestyle that will lead to better health and fitness. Are you an athlete or someone who already incorporates some sort of training into your schedule but are not receiving the results you think you should? This section will help educate you on what happens to the body when you exercise and what type of exercises may be benefi-cial to get the desired look, while at the same time become health-ier.

As you recall, good fitness and good health are two different things. The focus is to design an exercise program that promotes good fit-ness as well as good health. Since the main point of this book is how our hormones trigger our body to either burn or store fat, we will discuss which types of physical exercise trigger the body to burn calories from fat and which trigger the body to burn calories from proteins and carbohydrates.

Manufacturing Energy

All along we've been talking about the importance of burning calories from fats, as opposed to proteins and carbohydrates to succeed in any weight loss program. To produce energy, we must first break down fats, proteins and carbohydrates. The breakdown of one gram of fat burns 9 calories, while the breakdown of one gram of protein or carbohydrate burns 4 calories. Fat burns roughly two and a half times more calories than protein or carbohydrate. The presence or absence of certain hormones and oxygen will trigger which of the three are burned for energy. The breakdown of carbohydrates into energy is quicker than protein or fats, but the supply is limited. Additional steps are needed to break down proteins and fats, which are more abundant. All three will eventually be broken down into adenosine triphosphate (ATP), which is the actual currency used for the production of energy.

Imagine the way your body breaks down fat, proteins and carbohydrates to produce energy (ATP), as different types of financial assets. Think of carbohydrates as money in your checking account. It's easily accessible and can quickly be used as cash. It's limited in supply because you should have more stashed away in a long-term savings or retirement account, which is what fats can be thought as. If you need to tap into your retirement account to get cash you can, but it's not as easily accessible as your checking account.

The point is that carbohydrates are easily converted into cash (energy), while the money in your savings accounts, much like fats, are not as easily converted into cash. A good financial planner will tell you that you should have more money socked-away in a retirement account than in a simple checking account. The body is quite similar; we have more potential energy from the fat on our body, than from the available carbohydrates, because their supply is limited. All three forms of calories (proteins, carbohydrates and fats) need to be broken down into energy (ATP). This is where the similarities of our financial model differ, because we don't ever want to use money that has been saved in our retirement account, but we do want to use the fat stored away on our body for energy.

Continuing with our financial analogy, there is an exchange rate that comes into play when we produce energy (ATP). This is where exercise and the intensity level you train at can have an impact on the production of energy (ATP). One molecule of glucose is broken down and converted into either 2-ATP's or 36-ATP's. The deciding factor for that conversion rate is dependent on the availability of oxygen. It's definitely smarter to exchange one glucose molecule for 36-ATP's, than it is for only 2-ATP's. Therefore, the buying power of energy is greater when oxygen is available.

If the exercise intensity level is low to moderate and oxygen is available, the body will use "aerobic metabolism" to produce energy. This allows for the conversion of 36-units of energy. However, if the intensity level is high enough that it reduces the availability of oxygen, the body will produce energy by way of "anaerobic metabolism." This method is less efficient and only produces 2-units of energy.

The supply of oxygen is vital for the conversion of energy (ATP). This is why it is important to examine the intensity level of your workout. Depending on the intensity of your workout determines if there is oxygen available or not. Are you supplying enough oxygen to your muscles when you exercise? Is the intensity level of your workout producing only 2 or 36 units of energy?

One drawback for creating energy (ATP) without oxygen is a byproduct called lactic acid. Think of lactic acid as the "interest rate" that needs to be paid back. If there is a high accumulation of lactic acid, fatigue sets in. A high interest rate will wear anybody down. This is why it is important to examine the intensity level, because if you're only producing 2-units of energy instead of 36-units you may run out of energy very quickly. However, if the intensity level is low to moderate, which allows for the availability of oxygen, you produce 36-units of energy. There is no high interest to be paid; therefore less fatigue is experienced but most importantly we can burn calories from stored body fat.

Aerobic & Anaerobic Metabolism

The workouts we do can be classified as either aerobic or anaerobic exercises. The way the body produces energy while we do either of these types of exercises are called aerobic or anaerobic metabolism. Aerobic and anaerobic exercise is different than aerobic and anaerobic metabolism.

The term, "aerobic exercise" is a fairly common term, which most people are familiar with. Most people think of aerobic exercise as any physical activity such as walking, running, cycling, stair-climbing, aerobic dance, swimming for 10, 20, 30 minutes or more, at a low to moderate intensity level.

Anaerobic exercise on the other hand is an activity like weight lifting, sprinting, speed skating or any type of physical activity that can be done for only a very short period of time and at a much higher level of intensity. This type of activity cannot be sustained for long periods of time.

Aerobic and anaerobic metabolism is the process the body uses to produce energy. If oxygen is available, aerobic metabolism is used and the body can break down calories from fats for energy. If oxygen is unavailable, anaerobic metabolism is used and the body will burn calories from the breakdown of carbohydrates for energy.

One of the main problems for our inability to firm and tone our body from exercising is that many of us are performing aerobic activities at too high an intensity level which triggers anaerobic metabolism. In other words, we are doing aerobic activities such as walking, jogging, cycling, stair climbing, dancing and swimming at a higher intensity level than our body is conditioned for. Thus, our body is depending on anaerobic metabolism for the production of energy instead of aerobic metabolism. In which case people are misled into thinking that because they are doing aerobic exercises, they are utilizing aerobic metabolism. This may not be the case.

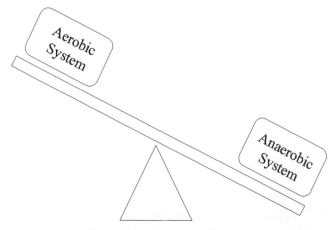

Low intensity exercise causes aerobic metabolism to dominate.

The body has two systems for producing energy (ATP). One system we refer to as the aerobic (metabolism) system, which means the body uses oxygen for the production of energy and can burn calories from fat. The other system is called the anaerobic (metabolism) system and can produce energy (ATP) without the need of oxygen and readily burns calories from the breakdown of carbohydrates.

Both systems are constantly at work simultaneously, throughout the day. If you are sitting around reading, you're probably producing most of your energy through aerobic metabolism, but if you are running from that saber tooth tiger your body will be predominately running off of anaerobic metabolism. As you begin to walk (intensity level increases) down the street your body will begin to use a little more of its anaerobic metabolism and a bit less of its aerobic metabolism. If you start jogging down the street your body will use even less of your aerobic metabolism and more of your anaerobic metabolism. What we will talk about later is determining the aerobic threshold or plateau (intensity level which is measured by our heart rate) we can exercise at that allows us to continually use aerobic metabolism.

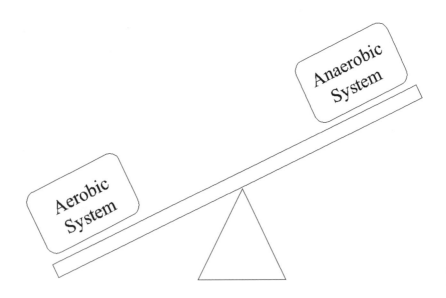

High intensity exercise causes anaerobic metabolism to dominate.

A major difference in these two systems is aerobic metabolism takes a little longer to produce energy than anaerobic metabolism. Just like the analogy about money, anaerobic metabolism quickly converts carbohydrates (checking account) into readily available currency (ATP), whereas aerobic metabolism utilizes fats (long-term retirement savings account), and takes longer to convert into energy (ATP).

Let's continue with the differences between aerobic and anaerobic exercise. Aerobic exercise typically means with oxygen, whereas anaerobic exercise is without oxygen. If you're training aerobically you're able to supply your body (muscles) with as much oxygen as the body is demanding. However, when you train anaerobically your muscles are demanding more oxygen than you're able to supply.

It's all a matter of supply and demand. If your muscles are demanding more oxygen than it can supply, you go into what is referred to as "oxygen debt." When you're in oxygen debt your muscles are dependent on anaerobic metabolism for energy. As we just learned, when there is oxygen available you can produce 36 units of energy (ATP). If you're training anaerobically, without oxygen, your body is only able to produce 2 units of energy (ATP). The exchange rate isn't as good when you depend more on your anaerobic system. Remember, the intensity level of your training, which is measured by your heart rate determines what percentage of your aerobic or anaerobic system is responsible for producing energy. We will discuss more about finding the proper training intensity to ensure our aerobic system is being utilized later.

Thus, an important piece of the puzzle regarding exercise and weight loss is the availability of oxygen. The reason oxygen is such an important part of this puzzle is because when oxygen is available your body can break down fats for energy. If there is no oxygen available, your body is unable to break down fats. Therefore, when you train anaerobically, without oxygen, your body can only break down carbohydrates and proteins for energy. If there is no oxygen available there is no fat breakdown! This can explain why so many people are not losing weight and firming up from all the calories they're burning when they exercise. It doesn't really matter how many calories you're burning, if you're only burning calories from carbohydrates and protein. The key is to trigger your body to burn calories from fat!

The last difference between the two is aerobic exercise is easy to perform as well as stress reducing, while anaerobic exercise is more taxing and stress producing. Recall that physical stress is another component that can exhaust the adrenal glands. It's possible your training routine may be contributing to your adrenal exhaustion, which leads to the inability to burn fat and lose weight.

How do you feel when you finish your aerobic workout? Do you feel good and refreshed or are you tired and fatigued? A good rule of thumb to use after completing your aerobic workout (walking, jogging, stair-steps, cycling, aerobic dance, etc.), is to ask yourself if you can do the exact same workout, all over again, at that moment. If you can say "yes," you probably trained aerobically. If you feel exhausted and tired after your aerobic activity, you may be training at too high an intensity level, which is making your body depend on its anaerobic system for energy and leaving lots of lactic acid in your system, making you feel fatigued. Since most of us working out aren't training for some competition but rather to lose weight and shape up, we don't need to be doing our aerobic training at an intensity level that it leaves us fatigued.

Training Intensity

Anaerobic metabolism is primarily dependent on the breakdown of sugars (carbohydrates) for the production of energy. Throughout the day, the body is continually making energy by burning calories simultaneously from both aerobic and anaerobic metabolism. Depending on the intensity of your activity or exercise determines if you are calling more upon aerobic or anaerobic metabolism for the production of energy. The goal is to use aerobic metabolism more than anaerobic metabolism, which allows the body to break down fats for fuel more so than carbohydrates.

The point to remember is for aerobic metabolism to function, "oxygen" must be present. When there is no oxygen available, the body is forced to produce energy through anaerobic metabolism. This means that if you are exercising at too high an intensity level, which requires more anaerobic metabolism than aerobic metabolism you're breaking down more carbohydrates and proteins (lean muscle tissue) for the production of energy and less fat.

At a low to moderate level of training intensity, oxygen is available and a greater percentage of energy is produced through aerobic metabolism. When we exercise at too high an intensity level than our body has been conditioned for, there will be less oxygen available. When this happens the body is forced to produce a greater percentage of its energy through anaerobic metabolism. When oxygen is available, we burn calories from stored body fat. When the body is called upon to generate a greater percentage of energy from anaerobic metabolism than aerobic metabolism, the body burns more calories from carbohydrates and proteins than from fat. Oxygen is the limiting or deciding factor!

The name of the game is to perform aerobic exercise at a low to moderate intensity level, which allows for aerobic metabolism. Thus, expanding our aerobic capacity to better utilize fat for energy. When we do this we will expand and further develop our aerobic metabolism (system) potential.

It is very important to expand our aerobic capacity because we spend roughly 23 hours a day utilizing aerobic metabolism and only one hour a day (when we exercise) utilizing anaerobic metabolism. Doesn't it make more sense to spend more time training our aerobic system? Our aerobic system burns fat for energy, therefore, train and expand your aerobic systems to better utilize fats for energy. One of the biggest problems many of the patients and athletes I help train is that they are doing aerobic activities at a much higher intensity level than their body is conditioned for, in which case, their aerobic activity becomes more like an anaerobic activity. They are over-training their anaerobic system and not expanding their aerobic capacity. Don't make the same mistake. Find your aerobic threshold and train within it. You will be amazed with the results.

Summary

Aerobic exercise
- Stress reducing
- Can be performed for long periods of time
- Supplies oxygen
- Promotes the break down of fats for energy

Anaerobic exercise
- Stress producing
- Can only be done for short periods of time
- Is performed without oxygen
- Breaks down carbohydrates and proteins for energy
- Produces lactic acid and fatigue

Aerobic metabolism
- Requires oxygen
- Burns fat for energy
- Produces 36-units of energy

Anaerobic metabolism
- Does not require oxygen
- Burns carbohydrates and proteins
- Produces 2-units of energy

Chapter Eight

Target Fat Burning Zone

We have all heard of the proverbial fat burning zone. But what is it? Is it different for each person? Are you training in your fat burning zone? Are you doing your aerobic training at too high an intensity level? Could you be over-training?

The intensity level of your workout is measured by your heart rate. The faster your heart beats, the more intense the workout. As you run faster, your heart rate increases. When you run slower, your heart rate decreases. Therefore, the more intense the workout the faster the heart beats.

The name of the game is to train aerobically and make sure that the intensity level you train at allows your body to supply enough oxygen. Thus, your muscles can trigger aerobic metabolism and burn fat for energy. The problem is that most people do their aerobic training at too high an intensity level, which triggers anaerobic metabolism. We tend to think that we are in better shape, aerobically, than we actually are. This causes us to train at a higher intensity level than we should. If you're aerobic workout is being fueled by anaerobic metabolism, you will be triggering the break down of carbohydrates and proteins for energy, not fats! If you're not getting the results you want from your training regimen it's time to start measuring your intensity level to determine if you are utilizing aerobic metabolism. The results may surprise you.

**Two people running at the same speed does not mean
they are exercising at the same intensity.**

Different Intensity Levels

We are told the fat burning zone is a range or percentage of our
maximum heart rate. This is true! However, each person's fat burning zone is different depending on each person's level of conditioning. The charts say a 40-year-old person will be aerobic if they
train between 55-85 percent of their maximum heart rate. That
doesn't mean that one 40-year-old who has been a couch potato can
train at the same target heart rate as another 40-year-old who has
been an avid runner for years and receive the same benefits.

If they both train at 75% of their target heart rate, the first guy will
probably be training at too high an intensity level and be dependent
on anaerobic metabolism, which will not give him the fat burning
benefits he is after. He will be adding more physical stress to his
body, which leads to fatigue, caused by lactic acid. On the other
hand, the one who has been training for years can probably exercise
at 75% of his maximum heart rate and still be using aerobic metabolism. He's burning calories from fat, he's not feeling fatigued after
his workout and he is reducing stress.

To determine what intensity we should be training at, we first need to determine our maximum heart rate. This is determined by subtracting your age from two hundred and twenty. For example a 40-year-old individual has a maximum heart rate of 180 (220 - 40 = 180) beats per minute.

Intensity level and aerobic metabolism are inversely related, just as aerobic and anaerobic metabolism are inversely related. When one is up the other is down and vice-a-versa. When the intensity of our workout increases our aerobic metabolism decreases.

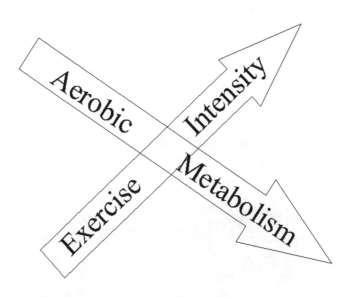

As exercise intensity increases, aerobic metabolism decreases.

A 40-year-old person may have a resting heart rate of 65 beats per minute, which is 36% (65 divided by 180 equals 36) of his maximum heart rate. As he begins to walk, his heart rate increases to 100 bpm, which is 56% (100 divided by 180 equals 56%) of his maximum heart rate. Since his intensity level has increased (from sitting to walking), he is depending a little more on his anaerobic metabolism and a little less on his aerobic metabolism, as compared to when he was at rest. When he begins to jog, his heart rate increases to 140 bpm, which is 77% (140 divided by 180 equals

77%) of his maximum heart rate. He's now using a great percentage of anaerobic metabolism and a smaller percentage of aerobic metabolism, all because there is less oxygen available due to the increase of the intensity of the exercise. If he begins to run faster, his heart rate increases to 160 bpm, which is 89% (160 divided by 180 equals 89%) of the maximum intensity his heart can beat. When he is training at this intensity level, he is probably getting 100 percent of his energy from anaerobic metabolism and nothing from aerobic metabolism.

The important thing to realize is that the intensity level determines which of the two systems will be utilized more. As the intensity level, measured by your heart rate, increases your anaerobic metabolism will be responsible for a greater percentage of energy than your aerobic metabolism. The more intense a workout, the greater percentage of calories are burned from carbohydrates than from fats. Lower intensity workouts allow for more fat to be burned for calories than carbohydrates. This is one of the reasons why walking is such a great activity for promoting better health and fitness.

Every person has what is called a maxVO2 or aerobic threshold, which is the maximum amount of intensity someone can train at and still have oxygen in their tissues. Once your intensity level takes you over this aerobic threshold your body burns calories almost exclusively from carbohydrates through anaerobic metabolism. As long as you train below this aerobic threshold, oxygen is present and your aerobic metabolism will function to burn calories from fats. The goal should be to train no higher than your aerobic threshold.

Confusion arises because each person's aerobic threshold is different. The thought that you can train anywhere between 55-85% of your maximum heart rate and be aerobic is true, but each person will have a different aerobic threshold. We need to find out where that level of intensity (aerobic threshold) is and train within those guidelines. If you're training above your aerobic threshold, you're probably not triggering your body to burn calories from fat, due to the lack of oxygen.

If there is no oxygen readily available while you workout, the body's ability to burn calories from fat ceases and the body looks for another source of fuel to burn. If all the carbohydrates are used up, (insufficient funds in the checking account) and there is still no oxygen available, the body begins to burn calories from the breakdown of protein (lean muscle tissue). This should explain why many of us are doing hours upon hours of both aerobic and anaerobic (weight training) exercise and not seeing our body tone-up. Are you doing your aerobic training at too high an intensity level that's causing the breakdown of only carbohydrates and protein? Are you over-training?

A common mistake that happens when people workout at too high an intensity level or over-train is, they often times breakdown lean muscle tissue instead of fat. This mistake can be quite deceiving because it is easy to assume that any weight loss that occurs is the result of fat loss. This may not be the case. Although many people will be happy to see themselves lighter the next time they weigh themselves. They could have been breaking down lean muscle tissue, which is heavier than fat and created a false sense of healthy weight loss.

We discussed earlier how eating a diet rich in carbohydrates could trigger the wrong hormonal responses. Eating a diet that is too restrictive in carbohydrates can also be damaging and trigger the wrong hormonal responses. There are people who are following a low carbohydrate diet and are exercising at too high an intensity level who may be unknowingly burning more calories from lean muscle tissue due to their training regimen. If you recall, carbohydrates are in limited supply in the body. If you are restricting the consumption of carbohydrates and are exercising at an intensity level that recruits anaerobic metabolism, you may not have enough carbohydrates in your body. Since the intensity level is too high and inhibits the breakdown of fats for fuel the body will begin to breakdown protein (lean muscle tissue) in order to create energy.

Therefore, a diet that is too restrictive in carbohydrates combined with the wrong type of training can produce the wrong results. Just because you lost weight don't automatically assume the weight you lost came from the breakdown of fats.

Patient Story

Thomas had been following a low carbohydrate diet for almost a year and was pleased that he had lost over 50 pounds. He had been running three times a week for 30-45 minutes and weight trained for 45 minutes three days a week. However, he had hit a plateau for the last three months and was frustrated because he couldn't understand why he wasn't able to add any shape and tone to his body.

After reviewing his diet and monitoring his aerobic workout we increased his consumption of carbohydrates by adding a piece of fruit to his daily diet and allowed an additional carbohydrate snack on the days he weight trained. We found that he was performing his aerobic training at too high an intensity level. Instead of running for 30-45 minutes and feeling exhausted, he began to walk at a pace that kept his heart rate below his aerobic threshold. He complained about having to exercise at such a slow speed but within two short weeks he noticed his energy increased, he didn't have that mental fog after his workouts and he finally started seeing some muscular definition in his arms and chest.

Thomas had been training at an intensity level that was depleting the limited amount of carbohydrates in his body. Since his workouts were intense, he was causing his body to burn calories from protein (lean muscle tissue) and not fat. His aerobic workouts were now burning fats for energy and not lean muscle tissue. This made him look leaner and he once again felt like he was getting some results for all his efforts in the gym.

The question we need to ask ourselves, are we training at or below our aerobic threshold (target fat burning zone) to ensure the break down of fats? Where is our target fat burning zone, which promotes the burning of calories from stored body fat? Are we doing our aerobic exercises at too high an intensity level, which causes the body to depend on anaerobic metabolism? When this happens we are breaking down calories from carbohydrates more than we are from fats.

To better understand the target fat burning zone, we need a basic understanding of how this zone is determined. The fat burning zone is based on a percentage of your maximum heart rate. A simple equation of subtracting your age from two hundred and twenty (220 - age = maximum heart rate) is used to determine your maximum heart rate. This is a general equation and is oversimplified by assuming there are no other variables that should be considered when assessing someone's maximum heart rate such as weight, medical history or previous training. It's simply based on the factor of age alone. It has been assumed that if you maintain your heart rate between 55-85% of your maximum heart rate, you are performing aerobic exercise and this will cause the body to burn calories from stored body fat.

Generally this is a true statement! However, as we just stated, two people with different aerobic conditioning can't workout at the same intensity level and expect to get the same results. One person may be burning more calories from carbohydrates and proteins while the better conditioned person training at the same target heart rate may be burning calories from fat. They're both burning calories, but are those calories coming from the breakdown of fats, proteins or carbohydrates?

The maxVO2, or aerobic threshold is our target fat burning zone. It is different for everyone and is dependent on the availability of oxygen as we exercise. The aerobic threshold is the maximum amount of intensity you can train at while maintaining oxygen in your tissues. If you train above that aerobic threshold or fat burning zone you have no oxygen available, which prevents your body from burning calories from fat. Only the most well conditioned athletes (marathoners and triathletes) can train at 85% of their maximum heart rate and still use aerobic metabolism for the production of energy. Since most people are not as well conditioned as these athletes, they should not be doing their aerobic training at this level of intensity (85% of maximum heart rate). You can train at 85% of your maximum heart rate, but that doesn't mean you are training aerobically and burning calories from fat.

The goal is to continue to train and become more aerobically conditioned. When you increase your aerobic threshold (maxVO2) it allows you to do more work with less stress. Meaning you will be able to walk, jog, run, cycle, swim, and skate as fast as you currently are, but your heart rate will be slower. This is a good thing and it promotes better fitness and health.

The aerobic threshold (target fat burning zone) for most people is about 70% of their maximum heart rate. If you've been sedentary, overweight, not working out and are poorly conditioned that percentage will be less, it could be closer to 55 or 60 percent depending on your current health condition. However, as you consistently train and become more aerobically conditioned you will increase that aerobic threshold and gradually raise that percentage a few points over time. It doesn't occur overnight but the more you train and better conditioned you become, the closer to 85% of your maximum heart rate you can train at and still be aerobic.

The assumption that we can all train between 55-85% of our maximum heart rate and be aerobic is true. Unfortunately for many of us, our ego gets in the way and we assume we can train at 80-85% of our maximum heart rate when in actuality we need to train at 70-75% of our maximum heart rate, or lower to ensure that our body is burning calories from fats. The other important piece of the puzzle is people don't realize they are training at that high of an intensity level. This is why I always suggest using a heart rate monitor when you do your aerobic training.

My Ego is in the Way

People will typically train at the higher level, thinking the "no pain, no gain" philosophy is the way to obtain results. I was one of those people and I let my ego get in the way because I didn't know whether to train at the 60 or 80% of my maximum heart rate. I always choose the higher percentage!

When I first learned about training below my aerobic threshold, I had to slow my running down considerably. I begin to use a heart rate monitor to measure my intensity level and was amazed how much slower I needed to be running. In fact, I hate to admit this, but I was embarrassed to run in public. I did not want anyone see me running so slowly. My ego was used to running at a nice fast pace. I thought I was a pretty good runner, but was I in for an awakening! The whole time I was running, I was depending on anaerobic metabolism for energy. I thought as long as I was doing an aerobic activity it must be aerobic. Was I wrong! I should have been running slower in order to promote the breakdown of fats.

The real eye opener came when I stopped to think about this training method and realized I was having to run so slow to keep my heart rate below 70% of my maximum heart rate. It didn't add up! Why were my heart muscles beating so fast when I was running so slow? Why did I have to jog at such a slow pace to stay within my aerobic threshold? Was I in that poor of aerobic condition? It didn't make sense to me, I thought I was in good shape, and I could run at a pretty good pace for 20, 30 even 40 minutes. Sure, I was tired afterwards, but I thought that's what I needed to be doing in order to see any kind of results.

Monitoring my heart rate showed me that I was training (intensity level) above my aerobic threshold (fat burning zone). I had to slow my pace down to a slow jog to stay aerobic, which was very hard for me to do. This made all the difference in the world. The intensity level (speed) I was running at was higher than my aerobic

105

threshold. In fact when I ran at my normal speed I found that my heart rate was beating at around 85% of my maximum. If you recall only those well-conditioned athletes, marathoners and triathletes, who have properly conditioned themselves, can train up to 85% of their maximum heart rate and still trigger aerobic metabolism. Unfortunately for me, I wasn't a well-conditioned runner and was always training anaerobically, which was triggering the breakdown of carbohydrates and proteins, not fats, for energy.

Within a few weeks of proper aerobic training I began to notice how much leaner I was finally getting. The extra layer of body fat that was difficult to get rid of was finally coming off. I wasn't tired and exhausted after my run anymore. I was feeling less fatigue during the day and realized I had been over-training. After a few months of proper aerobic training I began to notice I was running faster, while at the same time keeping my heart rate below the 70% aerobic threshold. It was then that I started to appreciate the value of training at the proper intensity level (aerobic threshold). Not only did this new training regimen give me better physical fitness, it gave me better health. Remember anaerobic training is stress producing and could be another straw on your camel's back, which can lead to further adrenal exhaustion.

The Heart Rate Monitor

Let's find out if we are training in our target fat burning zone by first measuring our heart rate. The best and most accurate way to do this is with a heart rate monitor that can be purchased at any local sporting goods store for less than a hundred dollars. The heart rate monitor consists of a transmitter and receiver. The transmitter is a band that you wear across your chest. It is designed to pick up your heartbeat. It will then send a signal to the receiver. The receiver is designed as a wristwatch that is worn while you train. The purpose of the heart rate monitor is to measure the level of intensity he or she is exerting while training. It is a great investment and I wouldn't do my aerobic training without one.

Target Fat Burning Zone

The next step is to determine your target fat burning zone or aerobic threshold. The old equation of subtracting your age from 220 and then multiplying that number by 55, 70 or 85 percent of your maximum heart rate does not take into consideration variables such as training history, weight, and health condition. You also need to have a calculator handy.

A simple and more accurate way to determine your aerobic threshold (target fat burning zone) was designed by Dr. Phil Maffetone. It's called the 180-Formula, and he found that if you subtract your age from 180 (180 - age = Target Fat Burning Zone), that number would be the high end of your target fat burning zone. This is approximately 70% of your maximum heart rate. For example, if someone were 40 years of age 140 (180 - 40 = 140) they would not train above 140 bpm. This would be his aerobic threshold.

When we try and consider some of the variables we discussed earlier in regards to choosing your target fat burning zone, Dr. Maffetone's 180-Formula takes into consideration some variables that need to be assessed. Two 40-year-old twins can't train at the same intensity level or heart rate and expect to get the same results, if they have different training backgrounds. Often times I see patients who walk or jog together, which is good, but they are at different levels of fitness. It's likely one person is in better condition than the other and they should be walking at different speeds. One person may be exercising within their aerobic threshold while the other one isn't. This is why it is important to use a heart rate monitor when you train. You may not be aware you are training too fast.

After you have subtracted your age from 180 you may need to add or subtract another 5 or 10 more points depending on the history of this 40-year-old person.

- Subtract your age from 180 (180 - age = Aerobic Threshold)
- Modify this number by selecting one of the following categories:
- If you have, or are recovering from, a major illness (heart dis-

ease, any operation, any hospital stay, etc.) or if you are on any regular medication
subtract 10

• If you have not exercised before, or if you have been exercising but have been injured or are regressing in your training or competition, or if you often get colds or flu, or have allergies
subtract 5

• If you have been exercising for up to two years without any real problems, and if you have not had colds or flu more than once or twice per year,
subtract 0

• If you have been exercising for more than two years without any problems, while making progress in competition, without injury,
add 5

The classic complaint I receive from people I have helped train is, "I can't workout this slow" and "am I getting any benefits from going this slow." The hardest thing is to get people to slow down. A rule of thumb I suggest you to think about is, if you have to run at a very slow pace to stay below your aerobic threshold I don't think you're in excellent aerobic condition. If your heart is racing at 85% of its maximum heart rate, but your body is only moving at 30% of your maximum speed, that's not good. The goal should be to have your heart beat at 70% of its maximum and have your muscles working at 70% of their maximum.

Patient Story

Joan was 54 when she began walking with her neighbors every morning. Her neighbors had been walking for some time and kept the pace fairly quick when they walked. After a couple of months walking every morning with her friends, she still hadn't lost any weight.

I felt her diet needed only a little adjustment but for the most part her diet was working well for her. I suggested she get a heart rate monitor and not let her heart rate get above 125 bpm when she walked and if it did she needed to slow down and walk at a pace that would keep her at her aerobic threshold. The next day when she walked with her neighbors she noticed that her heart was racing at 140 bpm when she walked. Joan didn't like the idea of walking by herself but she did and within a couple of weeks she finally started to lose a few pounds.

It seemed that Joan's friends were walking at a pace that was too fast for her. I often see couples walking or jogging together, which is great for company and encouragement. However, one person is usually in better condition than the other, which means one person is getting a better aerobic workout and is building their aerobic capacity, while the other is not.

My Mother's Story

I want to share my mother's story because it is very typical of what most patients and athletes I have trained experience. My mother, at age sixty had for the last few years been a steady walker and now had become a competitive race walker. She, in fact, had won so many trophies that she had taken down most of the trophies my brothers and I had won as kids, to make room for hers. As well as she was doing, she was still carrying a little extra weight and I told her, (very nicely) that the problem could be her training intensity.

I convinced her to start training with a heart rate monitor and found out she was training at a heart rate of 138 bpm. That is over 86% (220 - 60 = 160; 138 divided by 160 is 86%) of her maximum heart rate. Only well-conditioned marathoners and triathletes can exercise at 80-85% of their maximum heart rate and still be able to burn calories from stored body fat. Unfortunately, my mother was not a trained marathoner or triathlete, yet was trying to train as if she was. She was far above her aerobic threshold, which is one of the reasons she was unable to burn that extra weight off.

I told her she needed to walk at or below her aerobic threshold, which was determined using the 180-Formula. Her aerobic threshold was at or below 120 bpm, (180 - 60 = 120). She complained and said that it was too slow to walk at this speed and felt she would not receive any health benefits.

With the aid of a treadmill she started walking at or below 120 bpm. I let her know she could walk as fast as she wanted to, as long as she kept her heart rate at or below 120 bpm. She initially started training at a speed of 2.5 miles per hour. After two weeks, she noticed that she had to increase her speed to 2.7 mph to keep her heart rate at or below 120 bpm. Within a couple more weeks she now had to walk at a speed of 3.1 mph to keep her heart rate at or below 120 bpm. A few weeks later it was up to 3.4 mph; 3.8 mph; 4.1 mph. She finally started smiling! Eventually she started walking at 4.5 mph at 120 bpm. She expanded her aerobic capacity and found that to increase her heart rate up to 120 bpm she would have to increase her intensity even further. She was again walking at her original speed, but this time her heart was only beating 120 bpm instead of 138 bpm. Since her aerobic capacity increased, her body's ability to do the same amount of work became more efficient. Her heart didn't have to beat so fast to do the same amount of work as it did before. Now when she trains, more of her aerobic metabolism is triggered than her anaerobic metabolism, which allows her body to finally burn calories from fats when she exercises.

The hardest part for my mother and most patients and athletes to understand, is we may have been training too hard or at too high of an intensity level. It is very difficult to convince someone, especially an athlete, to slow down with their intensity level when they train. People are still believing and following the old battle cry of "No Pain, No Gain."

Aerobic Capacity

Training within your aerobic threshold increases your aerobic capacity, which is the maximum amount of work (exercise) the body can do and still provide oxygen to the muscles. As you consistently train below your aerobic threshold you steadily expand your aerobic capacity.

The best way to explain how our aerobic capacity functions is to imagine your red blood cells like little trucks with a cargo bed for carrying oxygen. Does your truck have a large or small carrying capacity for oxygen? The larger the carrying capacity, the easier it is to transport and supply oxygen. The more you train aerobically, the larger your truck's carrying capacity becomes. If each truck can carry more oxygen, because you are more aerobically fit, you don't need to send as many trucks. The trucks are dispatched by the heart with each heartbeat. If the trucks have a small carrying capacity it needs to dispatch more trucks (heart rate increases) as opposed to someone whose trucks have a larger carrying capacity (slower heart beat). This explains why a well-conditioned person has a lower heartbeat than an untrained or poorly conditioned person. Their aerobic capacity has increased making their heart have to work less. This is more efficient for the heart, because it has to dispatch less trucks (lowered heart beat). Therefore, expanding our aerobic capacity contributes tremendously to our overall good health and fitness.

How big is your aerobic capacity?

If you train at an intensity level that takes you above your aerobic threshold, you don't increase the oxygen carrying capacity of those little trucks. Anaerobic training increases your body's ability to operate under anaerobic conditions, but we spend approximately 23 hours a day in our aerobic system. Shouldn't we be training that system? The goal is to increase our aerobic capacity. We do this by training aerobically 3-4 times a week. If we train aerobically anywhere from 20-60 minutes per workout we expand our aerobic capacity.

Measuring your Progress

Once you have determined your aerobic threshold it will be important to measure your speed over time. If you determine your aerobic threshold is 140 bpm, you must do your aerobic training at an intensity level that keeps your heart rate at or below 140 bpm. To determine how much better your aerobic capacity becomes, you need to measure your training. The best way to do this is go out to a local track or mark off a certain distance in your neighborhood. Measure how long it takes to walk or jog a few miles or how far around the block you can travel for 30 or 40 minutes at your aerobic threshold of 140 bpm

Let's say it takes 30 minutes to walk or jog three miles at or below 140 bpm. Continue this exercise routine 3-4 times a week, at this same intensity rate. One month later go back and measure your time to walk or jog that same distance. The time it will take to cover this same distance at the same target heart rate may only take twenty-nine minutes. This is because your aerobic capacity has increased; you increased the oxygen carrying capacity. Continue doing the same routine for another month while staying below the target fat burning zone of 140 bpm. It may now take only twenty-eight minutes to do the exact same distance that used to take thirty minutes. This is a typical example of the benefits someone will receive from training in their target fat burning zone. The intensity level (heart rate) remains the same, yet our speed has increased. This progression will continue to occur as you train in this manner.

Summary

- Aerobic threshold is the maximum amount of intensity you can train at and have oxygen available.
- Well-conditioned athletes (marathoners and triathlete) can train at 80-85% of their maximum heart rate and still be aerobic.
- Most people need to train around 70% of their maximum heart rate to stay aerobic.
- The 180-Formula, subtracts your age from 180 to find your aerobic threshold.
- Increasing your aerobic capacity improves health and fitness.

Action Steps

- Determine your aerobic threshold with the 180-Rule.
- Monitor your heart rate with a heart rate monitor.
- Measure your aerobic capacity over time and distance and check it each month to see your progress.
- Begin training aerobically.

Chapter Nine

Exercise for Weight Loss

The best type of exercise or workout is one you will follow through with and enjoy doing. It's best to get a combination of both aerobic and anaerobic (weight training) exercise in your day. There is not necessarily one exercise that is better than another. The best exercise to do is something you enjoy doing. If you hate to jog, your workout should not include jogging because you will probably not continue that regimen for very long. If you enjoy playing basketball, tennis or soccer and would rather do that than jog, excellent. If you like to bike, roller blade or jump on a trampoline, these and any other type of physical activities that brings enjoyment and health benefits, are excellent. Pick any physical activities you enjoy doing; chances are you will continue to incorporate that activity into your lifestyle. Don't buy a treadmill or stair stepper to place in your house and use it only to hang clothes on.

The reason most of us are forced to follow some type of exercise program is because this is the only physical activity we get in our life. For the last several thousand years nobody really exercised, except for athletes. We can attribute the decline of our daily physical activity to the Industrial Revolution, because everyone was getting enough exercise from his or her daily activities. Back then we had no cars, we walked all the time, we carried things to and from and most of us worked the land. With those kinds of activities and demands, who needs to be spending additional time in a gym working out?

115

Today, most people workout and exercise out of vanity, not because of the health benefits derived from exercise. The driving force behind our workout routines is to look and feel better! If that helps our heart, lowers blood pressure, keeps cholesterol down, keeps blood sugar under control, reduces arthritic pain, makes us look younger, keeps our belt or dress size from getting any larger, fantastic! Many of us are working out simply because of the weight we've gained, the muscles we've lost or the muscles we've never had. We want to look and feel better about ourselves. Those are the real reasons people are exercising. If that sounds like you, make sure you get the return on your investment for all the time, energy and effort you spend working out.

Balancing Aerobic and Anaerobic Training

As I said before, good fitness and good health are two separate things. Let the facts be known, you can be in good shape physically, look great and still be in poor overall health.

To achieve your weight loss goal and add muscle tone and shape to your body, it is important to do more aerobic training than anaerobic training (strength training). *At least 50-70% of your training time should be dedicated to aerobic activities. The other 30-50% of your time should include anaerobic (strength & resistance) exercises.* This type of balance between aerobic and anaerobic activities will promote better health and fitness. Those who are poorly conditioned should strive to do more aerobic training (70%). If you're trying to add more shape to your body I recommend a workout that is more evenly balanced between aerobic and anaerobic training.

More often than not, people do more of one type of training than the other. They may do more aerobic training and not enough anaerobic training or just the opposite, to much anaerobic training compared to aerobic training. The key is to get a balance of both training activities into our busy schedules. Not to be gender specific, but oftentimes men prefer to lift weights and ignore the importance of including aerobic training. Whereas women will often choose to do more aerobic training and leave out the anaerobic training from their workout schedule. Therefore, people that only do aerobic training without including some form of weight or resistance training can create an imbalance in their aerobic and anaerobic capacities. Also, an individual can overdo the weight training and neglect the aerobic training, which also cause an imbalance.

In the earlier chapters, we discussed the importance of exercise to stimulate our metabolism. Exercise causes your metabolism to increase, which triggers the burning of additional calories. It doesn't matter if it is aerobic or anaerobic exercise, both will increase our metabolism. The reason is simple. Muscle tissue is metabolically more active than adipose tissue (fat). A pound of muscle burns more calories than a pound of fat! Therefore, we should be looking for ways to exercise the muscles of our body to help stimulate our metabolism. Are you using your muscles to keep your metabolism stimulated or do you only use your muscles to walk from the bed to the bathroom, to the kitchen, to the car, to the elevator, back to the car, to the sofa and back to bed? If that is the case, how are you expending any calories in the day and how can you expect to raise your metabolism if you don't stimulate your muscles?

When we start to include exercise into our daily lifestyle, we are making our muscles work and are creating additional muscle tissue. Please don't think that weight training will immediately give the look of the "Incredible Hulk." That will take years of dedicated training and dieting. However, this additional muscle mass (muscle tissue) that is being stimulated will burn more calories for fuel than adipose tissue. So, if you can add more lean muscle tissue and/or require your muscles to do more activity throughout the day, the body burns more calories. We can achieve our goals of losing weight and keeping the weight off with a good diet. However, if our desires are to add some shape and tone to our muscles, this will be dependent on including a good weight training routine.

Creating the Workout

The first thing you need to do is create a workout plan. Figure out how much time you can devote to exercising in a week. Can you workout three or five days a week? Do you have thirty minutes or an hour to workout in a day? Will you combine both aerobic and anaerobic training in a day? What aerobic activity do you plan on doing? What type of weight training routine will you follow? A good exercise program to promote better fitness (weight loss) and better health begins with aerobic training. At least 50-70% of your training time should be spent doing aerobic activities.

Secondly, figure out what your aerobic threshold or target fat burning zone is. Use the 180-Formula. Many people are going to be surprised how much slower they will have to perform their aerobic workout, but as you consistently train within your aerobic threshold your speed will gradually increase. Remember it is only those well-conditioned athletes (marathoners and triathletes) who can train up to 85% of their maximum heart rate and still depend on aerobic metabolism.

Third, start exercising on a regular basis! Whether the exercise is walking, jogging, cycling, dancing, stair climbing, swimming, skating or boxing, it must be done aerobically. If you do these aerobic exercises in an anaerobic state (too high an intensity level), you may not be getting true aerobic benefits. Remember, just because you're burning calories doesn't mean you're burning calories from stored body fats. Therefore, pick an aerobic activity you enjoy doing and do it within your aerobic threshold.

Aerobic training should be done 3-5 times per week. If you are new to the idea of exercising and have never incorporated exercise into your lifestyle, begin training only three days per week for a minimum of 10-15 minutes each day. An eventual goal may be to exercise at least 3-5 days per week for a minimum of 30-60 minutes, aerobically.

Those of us who complain how boring and unpleasant aerobic training (jogging, cycling, swimming or roller blading) is may be pleasantly surprised as I was. I know that when I use to train outside my target fat burning zone, I would finish my workout - happy that I was done, but, often times not feeling great. I was typically exhausted, from pushing myself too hard during the workout. Now when I finish my run, bike or blade in my target fat burning zone, I don't feel exhausted and tired. In fact, I feel quite refreshed when I am done. If you're not feeling refreshed when you finish your aerobic exercise, you are probably training at too high an intensity level and adding additional stress to an already exhausted body.

Progressive Resistance Training

Weight training or progressive resistance training is considered an anaerobic activity. Incorporating this type of training will help you reach the other part of your goal of shaping and toning your body. Over the past 20 plus years of weight training I have noticed that people who are trying to shape and tone the body often times don't start with a good fundamental routine that will get the most for the amount of time, energy and effort spent lifting weights. If you are new to weight training or are not getting the results from your present weight training routine, let's get back to the basics.

To promote good fitness (muscle tone) and good health, resistance training (anaerobic activities) should be 30-50% of our exercise time. Because time is so valuable for many of us, you must make sure that the exercises that you choose, will lead you to your goals as quickly as possible. Is your training time limited? Do you need to do four or five sets for each body part? Should we do exercises that work more than one muscle at a time?

Based solely on time, which is a major factor in determining if we can squeeze exercise in our busy life, it would be advantageous to do exercises that incorporate multiple muscles for each exercise. What is meant by multiple muscle action is simple. If someone is doing bicep curls or triceps kickbacks to firm up the upper arms, they are doing an isolated movement that is specifically done to target a specific muscle. An example of an exercise that is considered a multiple muscle exercise is the "pushup." The primary muscles involved in doing a pushup are the muscles of the chest, shoulders and triceps. In fact roughly 60-70% of the stress from the pushup is targeted to the chest, 15-20% is targeted to the shoulders and another 15-20% is targeted to the triceps. Understanding this makes it apparent why you should choose exercises that utilize multiple muscles, rather than exercises that isolate a single muscle, especially if time is a consideration.

A second rule of resistance training that should be observed is to train and exercise the larger muscles of the body first. The thigh muscles are larger than calf muscles. The back muscles are larger than the bicep muscles. The chest muscles are bigger than the shoulder muscles, which are bigger than the triceps muscles, which are bigger than our bicep muscles.

It's wise to design a routine that takes the size of the muscles being exercised into consideration. The reason we want to make sure we exercise and train the larger muscles first is simple. The larger muscles will fatigue and exhaust the body faster when you work them, compared to the smaller muscles. Therefore, don't try and do your leg workout at the end of your routine, because you may already be tired and those larger leg muscles will deplete what little energy you have left. Train the larger muscles first when your energy level is at its highest. It doesn't take a lot of energy to do a set of bicep curls, but it does take a lot of energy to do a set of squats or pushups.

When you exercise the larger muscles, you burn more calories! This is why you want to make sure you spend more time working the larger muscles of your body such as, your legs, chest and back, than the smaller muscles. Since our larger muscles are made up of more muscle fibers and tissues, they require more energy in order to function. Energy is derived from burning calories. Therefore, the larger muscles will be metabolically more active (burn more calories), than smaller muscles throughout the day.

Stress & Weight Training

The effects of stress on our body are far reaching. When you are constantly producing more cortisol in response to stress, you will be interfering with any muscle growth that you're after. Since cortisol promotes the breakdown of protein (lean muscle tissue), how do you expect your body to get the shape and tone you're after if you are constantly triggering your stress hormones to breakdown muscle? The lack of results you are after with your weight training may be due to the excess production of cortisol due to all the stress in your life. This is another reason why you must pay attention to the stress in your life and how you may be triggering hormones that are working against you.

If you feel that you are in stage two or three of adrenal exhaustion, it would be wise to keep the stress to a minimum. You don't want to be placing any additional stress on your body. Therefore, it is wise to eliminate weight training for a short while, until your body is well rested and you are able to handle a taxing weight training routine. If you are constantly exhausted, adding another physical stress to your camel's back is only going to make it worse. Limit your workouts only to aerobic training, which is stress reducing, until you properly rest and nourish your adrenal glands and overcome your exhaustion. Hopefully, within 4-8 weeks you should be able to return to your weight-training workout, as long as you take the necessary steps and reduce the stress load in your life.

Summary

- 50-70% of exercise time should include aerobic training.
- 30-50% of exercise time should include anaerobic training.
- Muscle is metabolically more active than adipose (fat) tissue.
- Stimulating your muscles with exercise will increase your metabolism.
- Exercise the larger muscles first.
- Cortisol promotes the breakdown of lean muscle tissue.

Action Steps

- Determine how much time per week you can exercise.
- Divide your workouts into aerobic and anaerobic activities.
- Exercise at least three times per week.

Chapter Ten

The Super Seven Workout

Let's talk about a workout routine that will give us the shape and tone we want for all the time, energy and effort we spend working out that also combines aerobic and anaerobic training. First, let's realize you don't have to train in a gym in order to do progressive resistance training. I will demonstrate exercises that can be done at home that will shape up the whole body. In fact, I typically train at home and only use my body weight for resistance. The workout I have outlined is pretty much all I do in order to stay in shape.

If you have a set of weights or access to a gym, you can do the same workout I've outlined. This workout is meant to work all the major muscles of the body. They are also chosen because they incorporate many muscles per each movement and can be done in as little as 15 minutes.

Squats – done with or without weights, targets the large muscles of the thigh and buttock.
Toe Touches – exercises the hamstring and lower back.
Calf Raises – done with or without weights, will work the calf muscles
Pushup or Bench Press – a pushing motion that targets the larger chest muscles, as well as the shoulders and triceps.
Chin-up or Cable Rows – a pulling movement that exercises the larger muscles of the back, biceps and forearms.

Abdominal Crunches – targets the abdominal muscles.

There are many other exercises that can be incorporated into your routine. These six fundamental exercises completely work all the muscles of your body in the shortest amount of time. Let's explain why these six exercises completely train every major muscle group of the body.

Leg squats - work the largest group of muscles on the body. We want to work them first. Leg squats work all the muscles of the thigh and buttock. A leg press and leg extension machine can be used instead of doing squats. The leg extension machine only targets the thigh muscles and does not stimulate the buttocks. Whether you train at home or in a gym you can do leg squats, with or without additional weight. Lunges can be substituted or alternated for leg squats. I typically do leg squats without weight and do 50-80 repetitions per set.

Toe touches - will target the hamstring (muscles on the back of the thigh) and lower back. They can be done with or without additional weight. Those who have access to a leg curl machine can replace this movement for toe touches.

Calf Raises - work the powerful muscles of your lower leg. If you train at home and want to increase the intensity, you can either hold a hand weight or do calf raises one leg at a time. I recommend doing calf raises on a step, which allows for greater range of motion.

Pushups or Bench Presses - develop half of the major muscles of the upper body. This "pushing" movement is a foundational exercise because it works half the muscles of the upper body. The muscles of the chest, shoulders and triceps are exercised when any type of pushing motion is performed. If you prefer to workout at home, do pushups. If you workout in a gym, you can do bench press with either a barbell or dumbbell. Machines that simulate the same pushing movement can be utilized. Modified (kneeling) pushups are a great way to lower the resistance for those of us who are unable to perform 8-12 repetitions.

Chin-ups or Cable Rows - this "pulling" motion develops the other half of the major muscles of the upper body. When you do a chin-up or rowing movement you exercise the muscles of the back, biceps and forearms. Doing a chin-up may be quite difficult for many of us. Therefore, you can do what I call **"hanging pull-ups."** In your doorway or at your gym place a bar about 3 feet off the ground and pull yourself up while your feet remain flat on the ground. The purpose of the "hanging pull-up" is that it allows those who are unable to pull their body weight up for 8-12 repetitions to redistribute their body weight and successfully perform 8-12 repetitions. It is a lot like doing a "modified pushup." Rubber tubing can be used to perform this movement at home. If you exercise in a gym, I recommend doing either seated cable rows or seated pull-downs. Both work the muscles of the back, bicep and forearm.

Abdominal Crunches - strengthen your midsection. They can be done anywhere and will help support the lower back. This movement isolates the muscles of the abdomen by specifically targeting only those muscles.

Secondary Exercises

Shoulder Press: targets the shoulder and triceps muscles.
Upright Rows: targets the shoulder and bicep muscles.
Triceps Press downs: isolates the triceps muscles.
Bicep Curls: isolates the bicep muscles.
Wrist Curls and Reverse Wrist Curls: exercise the muscles of the forearm.

Shoulder Presses are a powerful pushing motion that strengthens and develops the shoulders and triceps. This overhead pushing motion can be performed with a barbell, dumbbell, machine or elastic bands.

Upright Rows are a pulling exercise that targets the shoulder muscles along with the bicep muscles. This pulling motion can be done

with a dumbbell, barbell, cable or elastic bands.
Triceps Press-downs isolates the triceps muscles.
Bicep Curls targets the bicep muscles.
Wrist Curls and Reverse Wrist Curls targets the forearms muscles.

The secondary exercises should only be done after the basic movements have been completed.

How Much and How Often?

The best methods of increasing muscle strength and tone is with progressive resistance (weight training). The reason it is called progressive resistance is that we must progressively increase the intensity level in our workouts in order to stimulate the muscles to become stronger and firmer.

The intensity level can be increased one of three ways. First, add more weight to the exercise. The second way is to add more repetitions to the exercise and the last is to decrease the amount of rest between each set. Whichever is chosen, the intensity level will be increased, which places more stress on the muscles and cause them to become stronger and firmer.

Performing these basic exercises 2-3 times per week is all you need to do to get the shape your after. Now you need to figure out how many repetitions, how many sets and how much weight you should be lifting. A simple rule of thumb to follow, perform 8-12 repetitions per set for upper body muscles and 15-20 repetitions for lower body muscles.

A repetition is the number of times you complete a particular movement from start to finish. For example, if you do ten pushups, you are doing one set of ten repetitions. If you wait a minute after doing the first ten pushups and do another ten pushups, wait another minute and do another ten pushups, you would have completed 3 sets of 10 repetitions of pushups.

A second suggestion would be to do 3-4 sets of a particular exercise for the larger muscles (legs, chest and back) and 1-2 sets for the smaller muscles (shoulders, triceps and biceps). Always remember our larger muscles can do more work than our smaller muscles and the smaller muscles are usually involved in exercises for the larger muscles. These smaller muscles such as triceps and biceps are getting exercised when they assist in the pushing or pulling movement. Therefore, you don't need to over work these smaller muscles with the same number of sets that you would for the larger muscles.

The amount of weight you should use is fairly simple to figure out. Use the amount of weight you can lift for no more than 8-12 repetitions. If you are doing bench press you should be lifting as much weight as you can, so that you are unable to perform more than 8-12 repetitions. When you are able to successfully perform 8-12 reps on the bench press, it is now time to add more weight, do more repetitions or decrease your rest period to continually stress the muscles. Progressive resistance is needed in order to stimulate our muscles to become firmer and stronger. You do not stress the muscles to become any firmer or stronger if you do 8-12 repetitions and stop when you could have done 15-20 repetitions. This is an important sticking point for many of us who exercise and aren't seeing results.

What Is Our Weight Training Intensity?

One of the biggest mistakes I see people making in a gym is using the wrong weight when they exercise. For muscles to become firmer and stronger we need to challenge and stress them. We need to continually make the muscles work harder to stimulate them, otherwise they won't change and stay the same. What I typically see is someone doing an exercise, let's say bench press, and they are doing 10 repetitions and stopping. It is acceptable to do 10 reps if the tenth rep was the last one that you could possibly perform. However, most people will stop after 10 reps when they could have actually done 15 to 20 repetitions. When they do that, they never stress the muscles and stimulate them to become stronger and firmer.

How will your muscles shape-up, if they are not being challenged? If the muscles can already lift the weight ten times, they don't need to become any stronger or firmer. If we want to add more tone to our body, we need to stimulate the muscles in order to make them change.

Think of it this way. If you stop at 10 reps when you can actually do 20 reps with the same weight, you never recruit additional muscle fibers to come into action. It is like the muscles of your body are saying, "I don't need to get any firmer or stronger, because I can already handle that amount of weight that you want me to lift." However, if you make your muscles work harder by lifting heavier weights, doing more repetitions or decreasing your rest period, you now begin to challenge and stress those muscles. The muscles respond and adapt to that stress and become stronger and firmer.

Don't get the wrong idea that you will soon begin looking like Mr. or Ms. Universe if you stress your muscles this way. I am suggesting you train at an intensity level to get the results you seek for the time, energy and effort spent. If you don't stress your muscles to do more than they can already do there is no reason for them to adapt and become any stronger or firmer.

Does your training intensity stimulate muscle growth?

Patient Story

Susan was 43 years old and enjoyed working out six days a week. She would walk 3 times a week and lift weights 3 times a week. Her main complaint was that she never felt like she was firming her body when she lifted weights. When I reviewed her training intensity, I found out that when she lifted weights she never lifted enough weight to stress or stimulate her muscles. Part of her workout included ten-pound dumbbell curls, twenty-pound bench presses and 40-pound leg presses.

I asked her how many repetitions she was doing and how difficult it was to complete a set. She said, she would do 15-20 repetitions on all her exercises and the weights never felt heavy. She told me she could do more weight but was afraid that she would get bulky. I explained how muscles respond to stress and how they need to be stressed in order for them to respond and become firmer and stronger.

On her next visit to the gym, she took my advice and increased her intensity. She now performed 10-15 reps for the smaller upper body muscles and 15-20 reps for the larger lower body muscles. The next day she called and said it was the first time she actually felt sore after a weight-training workout. She kept up with her intensity level and six weeks later was able to notice a difference with her muscle tone.

I am not saying that you need to be "busting a gut" or hurting yourself on every repetition. What I am saying is that it is important to stimulate the muscles. This happens by making certain the last couple of repetitions are difficult to perform. Otherwise, you may not be stimulating any type of muscle growth to occur and are basically spinning your wheels. Examine your intensity level; do you use the proper weight in order to stimulate muscle growth? Are you progressively increasing the resistance in your workout? If you're not, you need to increase the intensity level of your workout.

The Super-Seven Workout

This is a workout designed to stimulate weight loss and build muscle tone. The principles behind the workout make it the most efficient and effective training routine for the amount of time, energy and effort spent exercising. If you can devote only three days a week for forty-five minutes to an hour to workout, here is a simple routine that will give you the results we have been talking about.

The first part of **The Super-Seven**, is 30 minutes of any type of aerobic training (pick your exercise: walk, jog, cycle, stairs, roller blade, swim, etc). This aerobic activity must be done below your aerobic threshold, which is determined by the 180-Formula.

The second part of **The Super-Seven,** are the six strength training exercises. These primary or core exercises will strengthen and tone all the major muscles of the body.

3-4 sets of squats
2-3 sets of toe touches
2-3 sets of calf raises
3-4 sets of pushups or bench press
3-4 sets of pull-ups or cable rows
1-2 set of as many crunches you can do

The number of repetitions for each exercise will be different depending on whether or not you workout at home or have access to a gym. Whatever the case, remember to do 8-12 repetitions for the upper body and 15-20 reps for the lower body if you train with weights. Progressively increase the resistance by either adding more weight, increasing the number of repetitions or decreasing the amount of rest between sets.

	without weights	with weights
Leg Squats	25-75 reps	15-20 reps.
Toe Touches	20-30 reps	15-20 reps
Calf Raises	20-50 reps	15-20 reps
Pushups	10-30 reps	———
Bench press	———	8-12 reps
Hanging Pull-ups	10-30 reps	———
Cable rows	———	8-12 reps.

50-100 abdominal crunches.

With time permitting in your workout schedule, you are at liberty to add to The Super-Seven, and target the specific smaller muscles with some of the secondary exercises mentioned below.

1 set of shoulder presses.
1 set of shoulder shrugs.
1 set of triceps press downs.
1 set of bicep curls.
1 set of reverse wrist curls.
1 set of wrist curls.

Each of these exercises should be done with 8-12 repetitions.

The most important part of **The Super-Seven** Workout is that you spend 50-70% of your time doing aerobic training. Secondly, you cannot add any of the secondary exercises until all of the six primary exercises are performed first. If time permits in your schedule you can add the secondary exercises to your routine. Third, we don't need to perform more than three-to-four sets for the larger muscles and only 1-2 sets for the smaller muscles.

Squats - Begin with your feet flat on the floor, toes slightly pointed out. Bend the knees and lower yourself until the tops of your thighs are parallel to the floor. Keep your back straight.

Toe Touches - Begin with your knees slightly bent, keep your back straight and bend at the waist and lower yourself. Try to touch your toes or the top of your ankles.

Calf Raises - With your toes slightly pointed out, rise up onto the balls of your toes then lower yourself. If you can place the balls of your feet on a step, it will increase the stretch.

Push Movement

Pushups - Arms shoulder width apart, lower yourself until you almost touch the ground with your chest. Modified pushups with your knees on the ground will reduce the weight.

 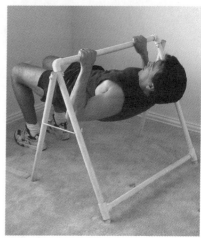

Pull Movement

Hanging Pull-ups - Start with the feet flat on the floor, arms are shoulder width apart with an overhanded grip. Hang yourself from a bar that is 30-36 inches off the ground. Pull yourself up until the front of your chest almost touches the bar, then lower yourself.

Or

Pull Movement

Wall Pulls - Knees slightly bent, with arms extended pull towards chest and pull shoulders back.

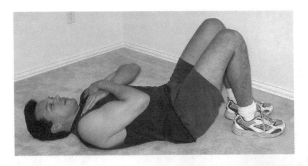

Abdominal Crunches - Start with your feet flat on the ground. Lay your arms across the chest or behind the head. At the same time pull your knees to your chest and pull down toward your pelvis.

Secondary Exercises

Overhead Presses- Press the weight overhead and then lower it to about eye level. Can be done either sitting or standing. Placing your elbows out to the side or the front will target the shoulder muscle differently.

Upright Rows- Begin with feet shoulder width apart. With an overhand grip pull the barbell (dumbbell, cable or elastic bands) up to your chin and then lower the bar. Keep your abdominals tight and limit the swinging of the upper torso.

Tricep Pushdowns- Feet flat on the ground, shoulder width apart. Grab the cable or elastic band with an overhand grip and push down to straighten the arms. Control the weight when it comes back to the starting position until the arm is bent around 90 degrees and then push on it.

Bicep Curls- With feet flat on the ground, grab the bar with an underhand grip about shoulder width apart. Tighten your back muscles and curl the bar (dumbbells, cables or elastic band). Do not rock or swing the body in order to do another repetition.

The Five or Six Day Workout

For those who have more time available or are more eager to workout and are hoping to speed up their results, you can train five or six days. Here's how.

Monday, Wednesday and Friday train aerobically for 30 minutes to an hour.

Tuesday, Thursday and Saturday weight training for 30 minutes to an hour.

Many times I find myself with only 30-45 minutes to train. When this is the case, I will do **The Super-Seven Workout** in that time. I simply reduce the amount of time I train aerobically and reduce the number of sets from three to two. I attempt to keep the same proportions of 50-70% of my training as aerobic training and 30-50% of my time doing progressive resistance exercises.

Why the Super-Seven Workout

These are two reasons why I feel these seven exercises are all you need to do to achieve a physique that is leaner and firmer than we have now. First, all our military personnel in boot camp only do exercises that require their own body weight. They are not working out with weights and they get in excellent physical condition by running and doing pushups, pull-ups and crunches.

Secondly, consider Herschel Walker who is arguably one of the greatest collegiate running backs who also had a very impressive and successful career with the Dallas Cowboys. Many people may have heard the story that as a teenager he would do a hundreds of pushups and sit-ups each day. He was known to have followed the same kind of routine as a collegiate, as well as a professional athlete. Herschel Walker did not spend much time in the gym lifting weights, but by following his routine regularly he developed a physique that most people would envy.

With those two facts in mind, it should easily be recognized that you don't need to be in a gym in order to lose weight and shape up your body. You just have to make sure that you regularly workout and balance your aerobic and anaerobic training.

Training Tips

Start with a good pair of walking, running or cross training shoes. If you have a flat foot or high arch it is important to be wearing the proper shoes for your feet. If you have flat-feet (pronator) or high arches (supinator) you should be wearing a shoe that is constructed to support the biomechanical movement for your specific feet. The two shoe designs are different. I see patients who complain of knee or hip pain that is caused by wearing the wrong shoe for their feet. Whenever you buy your walking, running or cross training shoe, inform the sales clerk that you either have flat feet (pronator) or high arches (supinator). If they don't know what you are talking about find a more knowledgeable clerk or go to another store. Remember, the feet are the foundation to your body. A good shoe does not have to be an expensive shoe, but it does have to fit properly and move in accordance to how your foot moves.

Drink plenty of water before, during and after your workout. It is recommended that we drink 8-10 glasses of water a day. If we add exercise to our daily lifestyle we need to be drinking another couple of glasses. If you are constantly feeling thirsty, that is not a good sign. That is an indication that your body is in a state of dehydration. The body prefers water. Coffee, sodas, juices and flavored drinks are not water. The kidneys have to work hard to separate out the water from the rest of the contents. Also, all caffeinated drinks such as coffee and most soft drinks act as diuretics, that cause us to urinate more often and leads to dehydration.

Warm up and lightly stretch before and after your workout. A good warm-up may consist of walking or riding a stationary bike for 5-10 minutes to get the blood flowing. One of the worst mistakes people make is stretching their cold muscles before they are warmed up or before they workout. Many times people arrive at the gym right after work, where they have been sedentary all day long. They usually proceed to the squat rack or bench press and quickly tug on their legs or shoulders to stretch or warm up. Since the muscles are not warmed up and are cold and inelastic, they begin to microscopically tear those muscles as they tug and pull on their legs and arm. Think of your muscles like a rubber band. Have you ever tried to stretch a rubber band that has been left out in the cold? It doesn't stretch very well, in fact, it may snap and tear. This is what happens to our muscles. I think dancers have it figured out! They spend 10-15 minutes doing basic movements to warm up their muscles and then proceed to stretch.

Get plenty of sleep (7-9 hours) each night. This is when the body repairs and rebuilds. We recharge our "batteries" when we sleep. One of the simplest and most overlooked aspects of any exercise program is our sleep and recovery. If you are not getting adequate sleep each night, it will catch up with you and this could be why you may always be exhausted. If we don't let our body rest and repair, how in the world can we expect our body to grow and become stronger and firmer? When we sleep our body releases most of our growth hormones. If you don't allow your body to properly recover you may be compromising your immune system as well as limiting any type of benefits from your workouts. Up to 20% of the benefits from exercise come from rest and recuperation.

Don't workout after eating! If you do, you may be turning off the Resting/Digesting mode and turning on the Fight or Flight mode while there is still food in your tummy. If you are going to do some light aerobic exercise this should not be a problem. However, for intense weight training workouts, sprints, spin, aerobic, or boxing classes, no food should be eaten at least an hour before the workout. If you workout within an hour of eating a meal, your body may still be digesting the food. As soon as you start an intense workout, all the blood needed to digest your food will be rerouted to your muscles. This inhibits proper digestion and creates digestive problems such as bloating, gas, indigestion and poor absorption of our nutrients. Certain foods digest faster than others. Most fruits when eaten alone can digest in approximately 20-45 minutes. Starchy carbohydrates take longer to digest than fruits. Proteins and fats may take up to two hours or more to digest. Depending on what you ate before your workout will determine how long you should wait before doing any anaerobic training. Don't make the classic mistake and drink a protein drink before going to the gym thinking that it will help you get through your workout. If you think you need a boost of energy to get through your workout after a long day, try some fruit. The fruit will digest rapidly and its sugar will be assimilated very quickly into energy, which is what you need to complete a good anaerobic workout. Some people who drink a protein drink prior to their workout oftentimes complain of intestinal gas and bloating. The simple reason for this is that the protein has not been digested and is rotting and putrefying inside their stomach. Another reason for all the intestinal gas and bloating could be the lack of digestive enzymes and hydrochloric acid, which is needed to properly breakdown and assimilate the protein in your meal. Still another reason can be poor food combinations. If you have a history of digestive difficulties proper food combining is essential.

In Summary

To Burn or Not To Burn, Fat is the Question!

In conclusion, as I stated on the cover of this book, are we burning or storing body fat? My goal at the beginning of this book was to look at some of the pieces of the puzzle that are being overlooked that could be responsible for all the weight gain and difficulty losing weight in our society.

I think we now have a better understanding of how stress can affect our hormones and that excessive, chronic stress can create hormonal imbalances. These imbalances can be why we have not had the success we have been looking for in our weight loss efforts. Therefore, the stress we place on our body is one piece of the puzzle that needs looking into if we are not reaching our goals of losing weight and keeping it off.

Have we exhausted our adrenal glands so much that they are not letting our body burn calories from stored body fat?

A second piece of the puzzle we need to consider is our diet and blood sugar levels. Our food selections are therefore another piece of the puzzle that needs to be considered. When we begin to analyze our diet with the knowledge some foods will trigger our body to store fat while other foods trigger our body to burn fats. We need to make better decisions with our food selections and maintain our blood sugar to promote healthy weight loss.

The last piece of the puzzle is the intensity level of our exercise routine. If our intensity level is higher than it should be, this can affect the results we hope to gain from our training activities. If we want to shed some of the fat from our body and replace it with some lean muscle tissue we must do the appropriate exercises at the proper intensity level to achieve these results. Look at the results you have achieved from your training program. The training intensity we workout at may be another piece of the puzzle that needs to be examined to achieve the results we want.

The puzzle as a whole, as I see it, is how can we become healthier? As I first stated, good fitness starts with good health. When we examine all the pieces of the puzzle and work at bringing them back in balance, our health improves. As our health improves, the body will not need to carry this extra weight, which is counterproductive and unhealthy. Therefore, I believe the success of any long term weight loss program is based on triggering the body to burn calories from fats and there are certain hormonal responses that occur due to the level of stress in our life, the type of daily diet we follow along with the type of exercise routines we perform.

Finally, those of you out there reading this information and are about to start following some of the principles, it is important to realize that these are lifestyle commitments and changes that can have a very positive effect on your life. Realize that some days you may not diet the way we talked about, but tomorrow is another day. Each week attempt to do more things that are positive for your health rather than negative and destructive for your health. Are you taking more actions steps forward than you are taking backwards each week? If you are, Fantastic! The goal is to always take more action steps forward in the right direction.

In Good Health,

Dr. Len Lopez

The END

Frequently Asked Questions

Q. If stress is the reason I am unable to lose weight, where do I begin?

A. If after adjusting your diet and exercise routine and you are still unable to lose weight, review the seven different types of stress that tax your body, and determine which ones need to be adjusted. If there is a large amount of emotional stress in your life, you need to find ways (counseling, meditation, prayer, deep breathing, bio-feedback) to control and lower the effects stress has on your body. If there is a large amount of any of the other stresses (internal, microbial, chemical, physical, electromagnetic or nutritional deficiencies) work to lower those stresses first, which will give you better health. When you are in better health it is easier to get rid of unnecessary weight.

Q. Is there a way to measure how stress affects my adrenal glands and my inability to burn fat and lose weight?

A. A salivary cortisol and DHEA hormone test is an accurate way to measure the functional status of your adrenal glands. Four saliva samples are taken throughout the day and tested. I prefer this test instead of a blood test for two simple reasons. First, cortisol fluctuates throughout the day therefore, one blood draw may not give as accurate a picture as four samples in a day. Secondly, the test can be done in the convenience of your own home. This eliminates the anxiety and worry of going to the doctor's office, which sometimes can alter the levels of your hormones due to emotional stress and anxiety.

Q. Why are cortisol and DHEA so important in a weight loss program?

A. Cortisol and DHEA levels are not only important for weight loss but are equally important in maintaining good health. When your body is under constant stress it produces cortisol. The constant production of cortisol triggers the body to burn calories from carbohydrates and proteins and *inhibit the breakdown of stored body fats*. The hormone DHEA has a positive affect on your overall health. It has been found to help with building muscle, burning fat, regulating blood sugar, increasing energy, vitality, libido and mental sharpness.

Q. What is functional adrenal exhaustion?

A. It is a term to describe what the body goes through when it has been excessively taxed with constant stress for an extended amount of time. When you are always under constant stress your body is constantly triggered to produce cortisol in order to protect itself. Your adrenal glands can only produce so much cortisol before they become depleted and exhausted. When this happens the ability to lose weight becomes more difficult and other health complaints can develop due to a weakened immune system.

Q. If my adrenal glands are exhausted, what do I do to support them?

A. Once you've determined which type of stress is burdening your body and have begun to lower that stress it is important to rest and nourish your adrenal glands. First, get plenty of sleep each day and supplement your diet with nutrients that support the adrenal glands, such as vitamin C, B-complex, pantothenic acid, zinc, magnesium, ginseng, licorice root, withania, cordyceps and adrenal glandulars.

Q. I seem to constantly be bothered by indigestion, bloating, gas, heartburn and constipation. Will this have an effect on my weight loss efforts?

A. Yes! If you are constantly bothered by these problems you are having a difficult time absorbing your nutrients and eliminating the poisons from your body. This can affect how well your body responds to a weight loss program. Digestive enzymes, good gut bacteria (probiotics), proper food combining and a good natural fiber supplement can help with these symptoms. Once these symptoms are eliminated your success on a weight loss program should increase.

Q. I've heard that a detoxification program can be helpful prior to starting a weight loss program. What is the purpose of a detoxification program?

A. A detoxification (de-tox) or cleansing program can be very helpful in a weight loss program. The purpose of a de-tox is to **remove** any harmful toxins that are in your body. I spoke of chemical stresses and how various toxins can interfere with the function of your body and your overall good health. Most de-tox programs last 2-4 weeks and are meant to flush-out many of the toxins and poisons found in your liver, large intestines, lymphatics and skin. The liver and large intestines are the major cleansing organs of the body. A diet loaded with processed food, junk food, pesticides, insecticides, antibiotics, preservatives, artificial sweeteners, prescription drugs, toxins in the water and air we breathe all have an affect on the functional capabilities of these organs. A diet loaded with fresh fruits and vegetables helps to keep these organs clean, which improves your overall good health.

Q. Isn't it important to count calories and fat grams in a weight loss program?

A. For thousands of years we have lived without counting calories or fat grams and have never had the problem with obesity as we do today. Of course, if you eat more calories than you burn each day, you run the risk of gaining weight. The goal is to eat a better ratio of carbohydrates to fats to proteins, in order to trigger your hormones to burn calories from stored body fat and not from lean muscle tissue.

Q. Is this just another low carbohydrate diet?

A. No! The main emphasis in our dieting approach is to reduce the intake of refined carbohydrates in order to balance our blood sugar levels. For years consumers have been told that "fats" are the problem and that we should eat "no fat" or "low fat" foods. Thus, the American diet has changed to include so much refined carbohydrates. Since a greater percentage of calories come from carbohydrates, we are triggering hormones to store calories rather than burn calories.

Q. How do carbohydrates, proteins and fats affect my weight loss efforts?

A.   A diet high in carbohydrates triggers the release of a hormone called "insulin." A diet with fewer carbohydrates and more proteins and fats trigger the release of the hormone "glucagon." Insulin inhibits the production of glucagon. Insulin triggers the body to store carbohydrates and fats, while glucagon triggers the body to burn fat. Therefore, it is important to have a meal that does not trigger a large release of the hormone insulin. Unfortunately, most of the calories in today's diet come from refined and processed carbohydrates, which causes a huge release of insulin.

Q. Do I need to exercise in order to lose weight and add some tone to my body?

A. Exercise will only complement your dieting efforts and speed up your results. If you are wanting to add some tone and shape to your body you will need to include some exercise into your daily activities.

Q. How much time do I need to spend working out in order to lose weight?

A. Ideally, it would be great to exercise 3-5 times a week for 45 minutes to an hour. If you are only able to exercise 3 times a week for 30 minutes that's a step in the right direction, the goal should be to start getting some physical activity in your life in order to help stimulate your metabolism.

Q. I thought you had to exercise at least 20 minutes before your body is able to burn fat?

A. That's not true! Your body is always burn calories from a combination of fats, proteins and carbohydrates. As you increase your exercise intensity (increased heart rate) you begin to burn more calories from carbohydrates and less from fats. It is when your exercise intensity level exceeds your "aerobic threshold" that you only burn calories from carbohydrates.

Q. What is the difference between aerobic and anaerobic exercise?

A. Aerobic exercise such as, walking, jogging, cycling, swimming, aerobic dance, in-line skating, etc are
- Stress reducing to the body
- Low to moderate intensity
- Performed for long periods of time
- With oxygen

Anaerobic exercise such as, weight lifting, sprinting, speed skating, etc, are:
- Stress producing to the body
- Higher intensity
- Performed for short periods of time
- Without oxygen

Q. What is the difference between aerobic and anaerobic metabolism?

A. The difference is oxygen! "Aerobic" means with oxygen. "Anaerobic" means without oxygen. The human body has a couple of ways of producing energy. If there is oxygen (aerobic) present, the body is able to burn calories from fat. If there is no oxygen (anaerobic) available the body is unable to burn calories from fat and is forced to burn calories from carbohydrates and proteins.

Q. How do I measure the intensity level for my aerobic workouts and what will it tell me?

A. Your heart rate determines the intensity level of your workout. As you increase the speed of your walking, jogging, cycling, swimming, etc. your heart rate increases. As your intensity level increases your availability of oxygen decreases. Oxygen is needed in order to burn calories from fat. If there is no oxygen available the body is forced to use "anaerobic metabolism" and can only burn calories from carbohydrates and proteins. The intensity level you train at will let you know if you are burning calories from fats or carbohydrates. A heart rate monitor is an invaluable tool that helps you monitor the intensity level of your aerobic training.

Q. Shouldn't I just concentrate on burning calories?

A. It is important to burn calories, but it is more important in a weight loss program to burn calories from stored body fat rather than from the foods you just ate earlier in the day. Wouldn't it be smarter to trigger your body to burn 300 calories from the breakdown of fats as opposed to breaking down 300 calories from carbohydrates?

Q. What is the "aerobic threshold" and why should I want to train below it?

A.   The aerobic threshold is the maximum amount of intensity you can train at and still have oxygen available in your body.   It is also called your "fat burning zone." When you train above your aerobic threshold (fat burning zone) your body will only burn calories from carbohydrates and proteins.   Therefore, in order to burn more calories from fats, it is important to train at an intensity level below your aerobic threshold.   This allows oxygen to remain in your tissues, which triggers "aerobic metabolism" and the breakdown of fats for energy.

Q. How do I find my aerobic threshold?

A.   The best formula to determine your aerobic threshold is called the 180 Rule. Subtract your age from 180 and let that be the maximum you let your heart beat when you train aerobically.   Depending on your current health condition you may need to adjust this number up or down 5 or 10 points.   Most people need to train at or below 70% of their maximum heart rate.   More details are found inside the book.

Q. How long should it take me to do a weight-training workout?

A.   A good weight-training workout for people who are not competitive athletes should take less than one hour.   A good intense workout with weights can be done in as little as 30 minutes, not including the time it takes to warm-up and cool-down.

About The Author

Len Lopez, D.C., C.C.N.

Dr. Lopez began his career in Dallas, Texas as a doctor of chiropractic. With a desire to treat patients with natural, complementary medicine he expanded his professional training and became a Certified Clinical Nutritionist (C.C.N.), Certified Chiropractic Sports Physician (C.C.S.P.), Certified Strength and Conditioning Specialist (C.S.C.S.) with additional training in Applied Kinesiology (A.K.) and homeopathy. He is an Adjunct professor at Parker College of Chiropractic and was the host of the TV show "Natural Health Made Simple." His approach to healing is very simple, "Treat the Cause – Not the Symptom." Dr. Lopez is an avid fitness enthusiast who shares his life with his wife, Melissa and their dog Samson.

References

McArdle, Katch, FI & VL. Exercise Physiology, 4th ed, Williams & Wilkins, 1996.
Guyton, A. Textbook of Medical Physiology, 8th ed, Saunders, 1991
Maffetone, P. Complementary Sports Medicine, Human Kinetics, 1999.
Baechle T. Essentials of Strength Training & Conditioning. Human Kinetics, 1994.
Murray M. & Pizzorno J., Encyclopedia of Natural Medicine. Prima, 1998.